The Seventh and the First

and the

The Divine Thread of the Torah

DANIEL LANGER

URIM PUBLICATIONS
Jerusalem • New York

The Seventh and the First: The Divine Thread of the Torah

by Daniel Langer

Cover art © by Joy Langer (joylanger.com)

Book design by Ariel Walden. Graphics by Daniel Langer

Printed in Israel

First Edition

ISBN: 978-965-524-087-0

Urim Publications, P.O. Box 52287, Jerusalem 91521 Israel

Lambda Publishers Inc.
527 Empire Blvd., Brooklyn, New York 11225 U.S.A.
Tel: 718-972-5449 Fax: 718-972-6307

mh@ejudaica.com

www.UrimPublications.com

Contents

Introduction

THIS BOOK IS dedicated to the memory and life of my mother, Sylvia Langer, מלדה בת הרעשל, whose selfless loving-kindness lives on in all those whose lives she has touched.

My mother was fond of telling this story of me as a toddler to illustrate my stubborn disposition. We lived on a third floor walk-up apartment. My mother was carrying shopping bags, and we were walking up the steps. I was slowly climbing the stairs behind her. When she got to the top of the third floor, I had two more steps to go. My mother reached down and lifted me up the last two steps. I walked back down and climbed those steps again, "all-by-myself." I think this trait of stubbornness has enabled me to engage in the tedious work of counting words in the Torah, and searching for patterns of sevens.

When I began this study, as someone who was returning to Torah, I struggled with my belief in the Divine source of Torah. I had been taught that the Torah is the blueprint of Creation. As such, every word and letter has significance. God and His Knowledge are One (see *Tanya, Likutei Amarim*, Chapter 4). To the extent that we understand His Torah, we understand God. I accepted all this with a simple naïveté. If the Torah is the blueprint of Creation, if it reflects God's absolute knowledge, then the intricate interrelationship of every word and letter has to have great import. When Rabbi Murray Schaum, the teacher who first taught me how to analyze a biblical text, introduced me to Cassuto's unveiling of numerical symmetries in the Torah, I became intrigued. Numerical symmetry could provide evidence of the Divine origin of the Torah text.

I began counting words that had a high frequency within a story. I discovered that words that appeared recurrently, and captured the theme of the section, often appeared in multiples of seven. This phenomenon occurred not only within small literary sections, such as within a chapter or two, but sometimes the words embraced large sections of Torah, demonstrating a unity of theme across passages that biblical critics attribute to multiple authors. For example, in the many tales of sibling rivalry in Genesis, we find the word *brother* in sevenfold repetitions, again and again, in each of the sections that tell the stories of these brothers.

Something else became apparent. When words appear within a literary section in multiples of seven, the *seventh* is connected to the *first*. Often, these verses will share other words, with the seventh verse completing the theme of the first. Sometimes, a word may occur for a seventh time over a wide expanse of text. For example, almost all the words in Genesis 32:22 are recorded in this verse for a seventh time (or multiple thereof), counting from the beginning of the Torah. Each of these words has an intertextual correlation between the first and seventh. (This verse will be discussed in detail in Chapter 7.)

On the Method of Counting Words

When I first began counting words, I did so by sight with pencil in hand, confirming my counts with Mandelkern's *Concordantiae*. Later, I acquired the *Torah Scholar* program, and was able to count words by typing in the letters of a Hebrew word and asking it to *find*, and then *find next*. Various spellings of words, especially verbs were checked separately. The *Accordance* program by Oak Tree Software was used to double check *Torah Scholar* results, and to search words over very large sections of text that appear too frequently to count by hand, such as *Abraham/Abram* or the Tetragrammaton. The *find* and *find again* system of counting with *Torah Scholar* was most reliable, and these were also used to confirm counts from Mandelkern's *Concordantiae*. Short passages, such as the length of a chapter, were done by hand and confirmed by computer. Counts are always based upon the roots of the word, unless otherwise stated. The verses of the counts are included, so that the reader can verify the counts (except for very long counts across the whole Torah text). When a word appears more than once in a verse, the verse number is repeated, corresponding to the number of times the word appears in a verse. For example, if listing the count of the Hebrew word for *light* in Genesis 1:3–4: "And God said, 'Let there be light', and there was light; and God called the light day," the listing would read as, "Genesis 1:3,3,4", with "3" listed twice for the two times *light* appears in Genesis 1:3. A semicolon separates chapter numbers. Also, when adding the Hebrew of a word in parenthesis, I will often write the root of the word, instead of the exact spelling.

On the Selection of Literary Units for the Counting of Words

There are a number of ways literary units were selected for the counting of words. Usually, the unit is determined by the various themes of the text, such as the Creation narrative (Genesis 1:1–2:3), the Garden of Eden (2:4 to the end of Chapter 3], Cain and Abel (Chapter 4), the generations of Adam (Chapter 5). The account of Noah and the Flood is a bit more complicated. The Torah portion of *Noah* begins at 6:9, but there are elements at the beginning of Chapter 6 that include the behavior of man leading up to the Flood. The *parashah* of *Noah* extends to the generations of Noah and the Tower of Babel story. Various combinations are examined for each of these overlapping literary units.

The chapter numbers, formulated by Christians often conform to a literary unit for reasons that are textual. For example, Chapter 6 begins with the prelude to the Flood, whereas the life of Noah begins at 6:9. There is merit in having a literary unit begin at 6:1, as well as at 6:9.

Very often, the sevenfold word patterns form their own textual units creating an intertextual theme for that word. When suggesting such a sevenfold word unit across a text that doesn't seem to be a literary unit on its own, in order to be valid, there must be a thematic connection between the first and seventh multiple, often sharing other words common to both. For example, *offering* (מנחה) appears for the *seventh* time in the Torah in Genesis

32:22 in the Jacob and Esau saga. The first *offering* occurs in the *offerings* of Cain and Abel (4:3–5). Both sets of verses share the exact word פניו, *his face*, again for the *first* and *seventh* time in the Torah. Both chapters share the theme of a falling out between two brothers. The first *offering* causes a falling of face, "and his face fell" (4:5). The seventh *offering* is sent in the hope of a lifting of *face*: "perhaps, he will lift my face" (32:21). The seventh *offering* becomes a *tikkun* (repair) of the first.

Sevenfold word patterns in the Torah form concentric circles of intertextual bonds, creating a mosaic of thematic units.

Symbolism of Artwork on the Cover

The tree on the cover represents the Torah, as a Tree of Life. There are seven branches, and seven roots. Three of the roots combine to form the shape of an *aleph*. The leaves represent words. Seven of the leaves are shaped as golden *zayins*, symbolizing words that are inscribed in the Torah in multiples of seven. Not every word is a multiple of seven, and those are represented by the many green leaves. Each *zayin* has a golden thread around its edges, connected to one of the roots. The *zayin* and the *aleph* represent the *seventh* and the *first*, with the golden thread of numerical symmetry interconnecting the leaves, branches and roots of the Torah.

Acknowledgments

I WOULD LIKE TO thank my wife, Eileen, whose love was steadfast during my struggle to return to Judaism, and who encouraged me to publish my Torah thoughts; Rabbi Jacob London and Dov Wallowitz, who kindled my awareness in my early youth of my need for Hashem and His Torah; Rabbi Avraham Weiss, whose living example, and whose outreach program – the Midrashia of the Hebrew Institute of Riverdale – has brought me back to Torah; Dr. Levi Baldinger, who gave his time and dedication to teach Torah to beginners at the deepest levels, and who helped return me back on the path of Hashem; Rabbi Murray Schaum, who has given me a peek through the keyhole into the depths of Torah knowledge (and who has given me a key), and who has taught me the method of biblical exegesis employed in this book; Rabbi Yehudah Fine, who has taught me Mussar – including the concept that one's spiritual growth in Torah must be reflected foremost in wholesome family relations; and for the countless other teachers of Torah, by word and example, including Rabbi Benjamin Hecht of Nishma, and the masterful teacher and role model, Rabbi Jonathan Rosenblatt of the Riverdale Jewish Center. A hearty thanks goes to the outstanding editing and layout staff at Urim Publications. A special thanks goes to my daughter, Joy Langer, who produced the artwork on the cover.

Blessed be Hashem, Who gives Torah to His people, Israel, and Who has been the Source of any Torah insights that have come to me.

Part One

Word Patterns in the Torah

Chapter 1

Numerical Patterns in the Torah

T HE TORAH BEGINS by counting – six days of physical creation completed by the sanctity of the seventh day.

> And there was evening, and there was morning, *one* day.
> . . . And there was evening, and there was morning, a *second* day.
> . . . And there was evening, and there was morning, a *third* day.
> . . . And there was evening, and there was morning, a *fourth* day.
> . . . And there was evening, and there was morning, a *fifth* day.
> . . . And there was evening, and there was morning, the *sixth* day.
> . . . And God finished on the *seventh* day. . . .   (Genesis 1:5–2:3)

As the Torah counts her days, it beckons us to count along with her. Through the process of counting, we begin to uncover her secrets.

The counting of letters, words, and verses in the Torah is an ancient practice. The Babylonian Talmud states:

> The early [scholars] were called *soferim* [see 1 Chron. 2:55 (Rashi)] because they used to count all the letters of the Torah; [*soferim* comes from the root *safar*, "to count."] Thus they said the *vav* in גחון (Leviticus 11:42) marks half the letters of the Torah; דרש דרש (10:16), [half] the words; והתגלח (13:33), [half] the verses. . . . R. Joseph propounded: "Does the *vav* of גחון belong to the first half or the second?" Said they to him, "Let a scroll of the Torah be brought and we will count them!"

> Did not Rabbah b. Bar Chana say, "They did not stir from there until a scroll was brought out and they counted them!" [*Kiddushin* 30a][1]

The Torah is suffused with word patterns. We can discover many of these patterns simply by counting significant words in a given text. The counting of words can be a valuable tool in directing our attention to parallel texts in the Torah, as well as a technique for understanding the simple meaning of the words before us. It is the aim of this book to demonstrate how the simple counting of words can lead to a more comprehensive understanding of the Torah text.

Significant Numbers in the Torah

Numbers play an important role in the Torah. Ideas such as Divine Providence, the mundane and the holy, perfection in this world, and the level beyond the natural world are expressed through the use of significant numbers.

One such number is *seven*. *Seven* is a number of completion and perfection, as in the *seven* days of Creation. The six days of physical creation are not complete without the *kedushah* (holiness) of the *seventh* day. Cain is avenged *sevenfold*, and Lamech *seventy* and *sevenfold*. Adam lives 930 years, one thousand minus *seventy*, which the Midrash assigns to the *seventy* years of David. Lamech lives 777 years. Terah begets his sons at his *seventieth* year. The waters of the Flood come after *seven* days, in the *seventh* month, on the *seventeenth* day. Noah takes *seven* pairs of clean animals from his household into the ark, and he sends forth the dove for periods of *seven* days. Abraham gives Abimelech *seven* ewes. Jacob serves units of *seven* years for his wives, waits *seven* days for Rachel, bows *seven* times before Esau, and is mourned *seventy* days in Egypt and *seven* days in Canaan. Pharaoh dreams of *seven* cows and *seven* ears of grain, signifying units of *seven* years. Jacob's family of *seventy* souls comes down to Egypt. Yitro has *seven* daughters, and Israel is promised the land of *seven* nations. There are *seventy* elders of Israel at Sinai. The Menorah has *seven* lamps. The silver bowl weighed *seventy* shekels, and many other numbers regarding the Tabernacle include units of *seven*. There are units of *seven* in the priest's examination of the leper and the plague on the walls. Miriam is shut out of the camp for *seven* days. The ordination of Aaron and his sons takes *seven* days. The altar is consecrated over a period of *seven* days, and blood is sprinkled upon it *seven* times. There are *seven* clean days that are counted for a woman or a man. The red heifer ritual incorporates units of *seven*. Balaam asks for *seven* altars, *seven* bulls, and *seven* rams. Yom Kippur and Sukkot are observed in the *seventh* month, and Passover and Sukkot are observed for *seven* days. After Passover, we count *seven* weeks of *seven* days until the festival of Shavuot, and after *seven* cycles of *seven* years, we come to the Jubilee year. Seven is a unit of completion and perfection. As we shall see, key words within literary units in the Torah regularly occur in multiples of seven.

Eight, that is, seven *plus* one, signifies that which is beyond time and space – the spiritual world beyond the physical. As such, we have the *eight* days of Chanukah, and the *bris milah* on the *eighth* day. The lights of Chanukah are connected to the spiritual light of Day One.[2] The *bris milah* brings the Jew to a spiritual level that is beyond this world, to the level of the *eighth*. The festival season ends on Shemini Atzeret, the *eighth* day from the start of the seven days of Sukkot (Numbers 29:35), when God is alone with His people.[3]

Another significant number is *six*, or *twelve*. Six represents the physical world, as in the *six* days of Creation. *Twelve* is a doubling of six, as six months of decreasing light turn into six months of increasing light. We can see evidence of the sexagesimal system in the *six* hundred years of Noah at the time of the Flood, the 120 years that God waits before the Flood, the *six* hundred chariots of Pharaoh, the *six* hundred thousand who stood at Sinai, the *twelve* wells at Elim, the *six* tribal names on each stone of the ephod, the *six* covered wagons, *twelve* oxen, *twelve* golden spoons, *twelve* bullocks, *twelve* rams, *twelve* lambs, and *twelve* goats offered by the princes for the tabernacle, the *twelve* spies, the *twelve* thousand armed for war,[4] the *six* cities of refuge, the 120 years of Moses, the six sons of Leah, and the *twelve* tribes of Israel and Ishmael.

There are many *sixes* followed by a *seventh*. God created the world in *six* days, and ceased on the *seventh*. We are to do our work for *six* days, and rest on the *seventh*. The manna was gathered for *six* days, but not on the *seventh* day. A Hebrew slave serves for *six* years, but is set free on the *seventh*.

The land is sowed and harvested for *six* years, but not on the *seventh*. The menorah had *six* branches pointing inward towards the central *seventh*. After eating unleavened bread *six* days, we are told to hold a solemn assembly on the *seventh* day (Deuteronomy 16:8). The cloud rested upon Mount Sinai for *six* days, and Moses entered into the midst of the cloud on the *seventh* day. *Six* signifies the physical world; *seven* completes the physical by adding a spiritual dimension of *kedushah*.

Thirteen, six plus seven, is the unity of both worlds. *Thirteen* is the *gematria* (numerical equivalent) of the Hebrew word אחד (*one*: א [1] + ח [8] + ד [4] = 13). There are many "twelves" which are really *thirteens*. The "twelve" tribes of Israel are really *thirteen*, when we include Ephraim and Menasheh, in place of Joseph. The "twelve" months are *thirteen*, when the second Adar of the leap year is added. *Thirteen* is the unity of God that can be found in the seeming disunity of the perceived world. The *gematria* of the four-letter Name is twenty-six, twice *thirteen*.

Ten is another significant number utilized by the Torah. We find the use of the decimal system in the *ten* sayings of Creation, the *ten* declarations at Sinai, the *ten* generations from Adam to Noah and from Noah to Abraham, the *ten* trials of Abraham, the *hundred* years of Abraham at the birth of Isaac. Abraham waits in Canaan *ten* years before taking Hagar as a concubine, and he sends his servant with *ten* camels in search of a bride for Isaac. Joseph sends *ten* he-asses and *ten* she-asses with provisions for his father. Joseph lives *ten times ten plus ten years*. The universe was created with *ten* statements, God strikes Egypt with *ten* plagues, and the Tabernacle was built in units of *ten*. Mystically, *ten* is connected to the *ten Sefirot* of Divine Providence, the lower seven of which interact more directly with the physical world.

Forty indicates a long period of time, as in the *forty* days and *forty* nights of the Flood, the *forty* days that Moses spent on Mount Sinai, the *forty* days that Jacob was embalmed in Egypt, the *forty* years of David's reign, the *forty* days of spying the land, and the *forty* years Israel dwelt in the wilderness. We also find multiples of forty to indicate large numerical units, such as the *four hundred* men that came with Esau (Genesis 32), the maximum of *forty* lashes meted out to the guilty, the *forty thousand* stalls of horses in Solomon's stables, and the *forty thousand* soldiers in Joshua's army.

These numerical systems are reflected in our physical world. There are *seven* openings in the head, and *seven* sections to the male body: a torso, two legs, two arms, a head, and the sexual organ. The female has *six* sections. Together, male and female total *thirteen*, the number of unity. The musical scale is not an arbitrary system, but reflects a physical reality. Each note is a given number of vibrations per second. Notes that are in harmony have a common numerical factor allowing the vibrations to reinforce one another. For example, the C note played an octave higher has exactly double the number of vibrations per second as a C note played at a lower octave. There are *seven* whole notes in the Western musical scale (white keys on a piano). The *eighth* note begins a new set of seven notes, each an octave higher than the first group, and each in perfect harmony with its corresponding partner. Just as *seven* represents harmonic completion in this world, *eight* indicates a quantum leap to another dimension, while keeping harmony with the level below. When we include the black keys, we get exactly *twelve* notes in the musical scale (a sexagesimal number), and the level above is the *thirteenth* – the *gematria* of אחד, the unity of above and below.

In addition to the explicit use of numbers themselves, key words often have frequencies that reflect numerical patterns. All of the numerical systems in the Torah are an integral part of its symbolic language. They are, to use Rabbi Umberto Cassuto's[5] term, the *golden thread* that binds the Torah together. This golden thread provides a unifying fabric within narrow literary units, as well as across disparate sections of the Torah, helping us uncover a rich interrelationship of message and theme.

Numerical Symmetry as a Tool for Probing the Torah Text

One aim of this book is to show how the power of numerical symmetry can point us to the myriad of interconnections that bind the fabric of the Torah. Observing the repetition patterns of the written Torah can help us uncover her secrets. When the Torah selects a given word to recur as a sevenfold unit, the Torah wants us to connect the *seventh* to the *first*, and to perceive the texts this symmetry binds as an organic whole. The Torah invites us to observe the unfolding of this word as it moves from the *first*, the defining moment in its life, to the *seventh*, its completion, and occasionally to the *eighth*, the spiritual leap beyond the natural world. When we study words of the Torah in this way, we uncover treasures that lie hidden just beneath the surface of the text. It does not take digging to unearth these truths, just the perseverance to count each word, as the Holy One, blessed be he, commanded Moses to number each soul that stood at Sinai:

> As the LORD had commanded Moses, so did he number them in the wilderness of Sinai. (Numbers 1:19)

Furthermore, we are explicitly told to count in units of seven:

> You shall **count** *seven* weeks of years – *seven* times *seven* years – so that the period of *seven* weeks of years gives you a total of *forty-nine* years $[7 \times 7]$. (Leviticus 25:8)

> *Seven* weeks you are to **number** for yourself . . . (Deuteronomy 16:9)

Although these verses are not about counting words, the concept of counting has been established with these commands, "*if you are able to count them*" (Genesis 15:5).[6]

It must be understood that not every word in the Torah fits neatly into a numerical pattern. However, when we *do* find repetition patterns within a given text, or across a wide expanse of text, it is not a haphazard event. When a word appears *seven* times within a segment of text, the Torah beseeches us to examine the *first* and the *seventh* and to connect the verses wherein these words lie. Through the study of the motif of each word, as it weaves its sevenfold pattern through a portion of text, we gain a deeper and wider understanding of the text as a whole.

To demonstrate the profusion of numerical symmetry in the Torah, we will begin with an analysis of sevenfold word patterns in the story of Creation. Within a given literary section, words that appear in multiples of seven express the theme of that section. Later, we shall explore the relationship of the *seventh* to the *first*, and reveal the intricate web of meaning formed by these patterns.

Chapter 2

Numerical Symmetry in the Account of Creation

R<small>ABBI</small> <small>UMBERTO</small> <small>CASSUTO</small>, the late professor of Bible at the Hebrew University of Jerusalem, introduced the concept of numerical symmetry in the Torah. One of Cassuto's passions was to prove the unity of the Torah, in opposition to those of his colleagues who held that the Pentateuch is an amalgam of fragments written by different authors. For Cassuto, numerical symmetry is the *golden thread* that binds the Torah together, serving as convincing proof of its unity.

If we count repetitions of words within paragraphs or larger literary sections of the Torah, we can discern clear patterns based on the number *seven*, or *multiples of seven*. To illustrate, we will examine the very first section of the Torah – the seven days of Creation (Genesis 1:1–2:3).[7] We will begin with Cassuto's numerical analysis, and follow with some additions of our own.

In his brilliant analysis of the story of Creation, Cassuto notes the following:[8]

(1) The account of Creation is divided into *seven* paragraphs, one for each day.

(2) The name of *God* (אלקים) is written *thirty-five* times, that is, five times seven.[9]

(3) The word ארץ, *earth/land*, appears *twenty-one* times, three times seven.

(4) The expression ויאמר אלקים, *and God said*, recurs *ten* times in the sec-

God אלקים
Genesis 1:1, 2, 3, 4, 4, 5, 6, 7, 8, 9, 10, 10, 11, 12, 14, 16, 17, 18, 20, 21, 21, 22, 24, 25, 25, 26, 27, 27, 28, 28, 29, 31; 2:2, 3, 3

earth/land ארץ
1:1, 2, 10, 11, 11, 12, 15, 17, 20, 22, 24, 24, 25, 26, 26, 28, 28, 29, 30, 30; 2:1

**ויאמר אלקים
and God said**
1:3, 6, 9, 11, 14, 20,
22, 26, 28, 29

**על־הארץ
on the earth**
1:11, 15, 17, 20, 26,
28, 30

water מים
1:6, 6, 6, 7, 7, 9, 10

good טוב
1: 4, 10, 12, 18, 21,
25, 31

day יום
1:5, 5, 8, 13, 14, 14,
16, 18, 19, 23, 31;
2:2, 2, 3

bird/fly עוף
1:20, 20, 21, 22, 26,
28, 30

crawl רמש
1:21, 24, 25, 26, 26,
28, 30

**after its למינה
kind (animals)**
1:21, 21, 24, 24, 25,
25, 25

**וירא אלקים ... טוב
and God saw
... good**
1:4, 10, 12, 18, 21,
25, 31

all/every כל
1:21, 21, 25, 26, 26,
28, 29, 29, 29, 30,
30, 30, 30, 31

tion – *seven* in relation to the natural world, and *three* (a number of emphasis) in relation to man.

(5) The expression על־הארץ, *on the earth*, is recorded *seven* times.

(6) *Water*, מים, is found *seven* times in Days Two and Three, which describe the division of the waters and the gathering of the seas.

(7) *Good* (טוב) recurs *seven* times, the seventh time as *very good*.

(8) Within the *seventh* paragraph, which deals with the *seventh* day, there occur three consecutive sentences, three for emphasis, each of which consists of *seven* words containing the expression *the seventh day*:

ויכל אלקים ביום השביעי מלאכתו אשר עשה
וישבת ביום השביעי מכל מלאכתו אשר עשה
ויברך אלקים את יום השביעי ויקדש אתו

And God finished on *the seventh day* His work which He had made.
And He ceased *on the seventh day* from all His work which He had made.
And God blessed את *the seventh day* and hallowed it[10]

(9) The first verse in the Torah has *seven* words.

(10) The second verse has fourteen words – twice *seven*.

(11) The *seventh* paragraph totals *thirty-five* words – five times *seven*.

In addition to the list above that has been gleaned from Cassuto's *Commentary on Genesis I*, the following additional items amplify the significance of *seven* in the story of Creation:

(12) The word *day* (יום) occurs *fourteen* times.

(13) The root of the word *bird/fly* (עוף) is found *seven* times.

(14) *Crawl* (רמש) is written *seven* times.

(15) The word for *after its/their kind,* (למינה, למינו, למינהו, למינהם) is written three times in the third paragraph in relation to the plant kingdom (1:11,12,12), and *seven* times in the fifth and sixth paragraphs, in relation to the animal kingdom. This word appears *seven* more times in Genesis, all in regard to the animals of Noah's ark (6:20, 20, 20; 7:14, 14, 14, 14).

(16) The phrase *and God saw ... good* (וירא אלקים ... טוב) recurs *seven* times.

(17) The word כל, *all/every*, occurs *fourteen* times in chapter one. The *fourteenth* appearance of *all/every* is written in the same verse as the

seventh occurrence of the expression *and God saw . . . good*: "And God saw **all** that He had made, and, behold, it was very **good**" (1:31).

In addition to the sevenfold word patterns listed above,[11] we also find numerical symmetry based on sevens in the number of letters and words in many of the verses.

(18) The first verse of the first paragraph has *28* letters, and it is divided by the Masoretic *trup* (cantillation marks) into two distinct parts of *14* letters each:

In the beginning, God created, בראשית ברא אלקים [twice *seven* letters]

the heavens and the earth, את השמים ואת הארץ [twice *seven* letters].

(19) The last verse of the first paragraph has *49* letters, *seven* times *seven*:

ויקרא אלקים לאור יום ולחשך קרא לילה ויהי־ערב ויהי־בקר יום אחד

And God called to the light day, and to the darkness He called night; and there was evening, and there was morning, one day.

(Genesis 1:5)

(20) In Day One, the sum of the letters of the first verse (28) and the last verse (49) total *77* letters.

(21) There are *seven* hyphenated words in the first paragraph.

(22) The words in Day One form a perfect symmetry of *sixes* and *sevens*. The first verse has *seven* words; the second verse *twice seven*. The third verse has *six* words; the fourth verse *twice six*. The last verse has two parts. The first part – *and God called the light day, and the darkness He called night* – has *seven* words. The second part – *and there was evening, and there was morning, one day* – has *six* words. The pattern of words in Day One is: *7 . . . twice 7, 6 . . . twice 6, 7/6.*

(23) There are *fourteen* letters in the refrain: *And God saw that it was good,* וירא אלקים כי־טוב.

Forty-nine, or *seven squared,* is an intensification of the perfection of seven. This number is emphasized frequently in the Creation story.

(24) As noted above, the Hebrew letters in the last verse of Day One total 49. The letters in the first clause of Genesis 1:14 total 49, as well. Both are related:

And God called to the *light day*, and to the darkness He called *night*; and there was evening, and there was morning, one day. (1:5) [49 Hebrew letters]

And God said, Let there be *lights* in the firmament of heaven to divide between the *day* and between the *night*. (1:14) [49 Hebrew letters]

Both forty-nine-letter sentences deal with *light* and the division of *day* and *night*.

(25) The Hebrew letters in Genesis 1:10 total 49, as well as the letters in the first clause of verse 28. Again, these sentences are related. In verse 10, God names the dry land *earth*; in verse 28, God tells man his role in relation to the *earth*:

And God called the dry land *Earth*; and the gathering together of the waters He called Seas; and God saw that it was good. (1:10)

And God blessed them, and God said to them, "Be fruitful, and multiply, and replenish the *Earth*, and subdue it." (1:28)

Man has dominion over the dry land, which God formed on the second day. The total of *forty-nine* letters in each clause underscores the association.

These *forty-nine* letter pairs move from the creation of light to the bearers of light, from the creation of dry land to human dominion over the land. The heavenly orbs dominate light, and man dominates the earth.

(26) The fourth paragraph, which tells of the formation of the bearers of light, has 298 letters: $2(10^2 + 7^2)$.

(27) The sixth paragraph, which tells of the creation of Man and his responsibility for the earth, has 549 letters: $5(10^2) + 7^2$, and 149 words: $10^2 + 7^2$.

(28) The numerical value of the verb *created* is 203 (7×29). The numerical value of the three nouns – *the earth*, *the heavens*, and *God* – total 777.[12] The total numerical value for the subject, verb, and objects of the first sentence in the Torah – *God, created, the heavens,* and *the earth* – is

980, which factors out to twice $7 \times 7 \times 10$, or $7^2(10) + 7^2(10)$.

(29) The total number of words in the seven days of Creation is 469, which equals $7(67)$, or $7(6)(10) + 7^2$. The product of seven, six and ten, all significant numbers, is supplemented by seven squared. All these significant numbers appear in perfect symmetry when we count the total of all the words in the Creation narrative.

There can be no doubt that a numerical symmetry based on the number seven exists in the first section of the Torah. This symmetry persists throughout the Torah, but it is most intense in the story of the seven days of Creation. As Cassuto said after his numerical analysis of the Creation text, "To suppose that all this is mere coincidence is not possible."[13]

In the Beginning God Created the Twenty-two Letters

There is a tradition that before Creation God created the spiritual *aleph-bet*. The Hebrew letters represent the twenty-two spiritual forces with which the world was created. The Torah begins with *seven* Hebrew words and four times *seven* Hebrew letters:

בראשית ברא אלקים את השמים ואת הארץ

In the beginning God created את the heavens and את the earth.

If we read the first four words as a unit, we can derive another meaning: *In the beginning God created* את, the letters from *aleph* to *tav*, the twenty-two spiritual forces of the Hebrew *aleph-bet*. Rendering the whole sentence in this manner we get, *In the beginning God created* את *of the heavens and* את *of the earth*, the spiritual letters of the heavens, and the physical letters of our text.

To confirm the importance of the word את, I counted the number of times it appears in the Creation narrative. The little word את made of the first and last letters of the twenty-two letters of the Hebrew *aleph-bet*, appears *twenty-eight* times in the Creation narrative.

Furthermore, note the following extraordinary pattern. The first *aleph* (א) in the Torah, in the word בראשית (in the beginning), begins a twenty-two letter string ending in the letter *tav* (ת) – the last letter of the *aleph-*

את
Genesis 1:1, 1, 4,
7, 16, 16, 16, 16, 17,
21, 21, 21, 22, 22,
25, 25, 25, 27, 27,
27, 28, 28, 29, 29,
30, 31; 2:3, 3

bet. How many twenty-two-letter strings beginning with *aleph* and ending with *tav* are there in this section? In Genesis 1, there are exactly *seven* cases. Taking the Creation stories together, Genesis 1–3, we have exactly *twenty-two* cases.

It has been taught that the Torah is the blueprint of Creation. As such, every word and letter has significance. God and His Knowledge are One.[14] To the extent that we understand His Torah, we understand God. Numerical symmetry is the imprint of the Divine engraved in the body of the Torah text.

For anyone who has long studied Torah, the Divine source is self-evident. However, numerical symmetry serves a much greater function. It is a tool for uncovering the meaning of the text itself. In literary units having symmetries based on the number seven, the seventh is connected to and completes the first. Sometimes, the first and seventh appearances of a word in the Torah come from seemingly unrelated texts, texts that biblical critics assign to different authors. However, the first and seventh are interrelated: the context of the *first* defines the essential meaning of the word, the *seventh* brings the word to completion, and the *eighth* is *l'maalah hatevah,* at a level beyond the physical world.

Chapter 3

Applying Numerical Symmetry to the Study of the Torah Text

A s a stylistic device, numerical symmetry is very beautiful. As a unifying factor, it is very powerful. But it means much more. The Torah is drawing our attention to these sevenfold repetitions in order to teach us something. Simply by counting, we can discover things that we might otherwise overlook. In this chapter, we shall explore various applications of word repetition patterns based on multiples of seven.

The Sevenfold Appearances of the Same Word across Many Sections of the Torah

At times, a particular key word occurs in multiples of seven across many different sections of text. When this occurs, the Torah wants us to connect the themes associated with this word from one section of the Torah to another. A very good example of this phenomenon is the word *brother. Brother* occurs *seven* times in the story of Cain and Abel, *twice seven* times in the part of *Parashat Toldot* that deals with the struggle between Jacob and Esau, *seven* times when Jacob has to face Esau again in *Parashat Vayishlach, thrice seven* times in the story of the selling of Joseph, *seven* times when the brothers return to Joseph's house and Judah intercedes on behalf of Benjamin, *twice seven* times when Joseph reveals himself to his brothers and reunites with his father, and *seven* times when Joseph presents his father and his brothers to Pharaoh in order to provide for their sustenance.

Surely, all this is not coincidental. Through these sevenfold repetitions of the word *brother*, the Torah is beckoning us to connect these stories of sibling rivalry. The development is straightforward: brother kills brother; brother wants to kill brother, but in the end they embrace and separate; brothers consider killing a brother, but in the end they embrace and remain somewhat connected. As we shall see, there are multiple numerical symmetries that unite these diverse brother narratives into an integrated ongoing theme.

* * *

The word *voice* (קול) appears *seven* times in *Parashat Toldot*, and *seven* times in the narratives of the revelation at Sinai in both the books of Exodus and Deuteronomy. This symmetry of "voice" suggests a relationship between the stories of Isaac and Rebekah's children and the revelation at Sinai. We will explore this interrelationship in Chapter 6.

voice   קול
(Toldot)
Genesis 26:5;
27:8, 13, 22, 22,
38, 43

voice   קול
(Exodus)
Exodus 19:5, 16,
16, 19, 19; 20:15, 15

voice   קול
(Deuteronomy)
5:19, 20, 21, 22, 23,
25, 25

The Seventh as a Number of Completion

Within literary sections, key words often occur in multiples of seven, the last of which completes a unit. When we follow the sentences in which these words live, we get a full sense of the essence of the text from the aspect of those words. *Seven* is a number of completion, and a literary unit containing a sevenfold appearance of a word completes the theme associated with that word.

For example, let us examine the sevenfold recurrence of the words *saw* (וירא) and *good* (טוב) in the first chapter of Genesis:

(1)   And God *saw* the light that it was *good*.

(2)   And God called the dry land Earth; and the gathering together of the waters He called Seas; and God *saw* that it was *good*.

(3)   And the earth brought forth vegetation . . . And God *saw* that this was *good*.

(4)   And God set them in the dome of the heavens to give light upon the earth, . . . and God *saw* that it was *good*.

(5)   And God created the great sea-giants and every living being that

creeps, with which the waters teemed after their kinds; and all winged fowl of every kind. And God *saw* that it was *good*.

(6) And God made the beasts of the earth after their kind, and cattle after their kind, and every thing that creeps upon the earth after its kind; and God *saw* that it was *good*.

(7) And God *saw* [after the creation of Man] everything that He had made, and behold, it was *very good*.

The seventh *saw . . . good* culminates in a state of completion: "And God *saw . . .* it was *very good*."

By following these verses, one gets a sense of the good within all the elements of creation, one element after another. At the end of physical creation, at its seventh appearance, *good* reaches completion. (However, as the Torah relates in the next section, Man would bring evil into the *very good* world that God had made. Man does not get a separate verse declaring his goodness. Instead, he is subsumed within the general rubric, "and God *saw* everything that he had made, and behold it was very *good*." In the end, even Man is included within the *very good* that God sees, but Man will have to earn this good and overcome his dual nature.)

* * *

The word *God*, the subject of the first verse, reaches completion on the Sabbath day in its thirty-fifth (5×7th) occurrence:

And God blessed the seventh *day* and sanctified it because on it He abstained from all His work, which *God* created to make.

(Genesis 2:3)

Godliness reaches completion not on the sixth day, but through the spirituality of the seventh. Time, as expressed in the concept of *day*, reaches completion here too, for this final verse in the account of creation marks the twice seventh time *day* is written in the Torah.

Convergence of Words Appearing for a Seventh Time in a Single Verse

Within a literary section, key words are found very often in multiples of seven, the last of which relates to the first. Occasionally, we find the seventh appearances of a cluster of words in a single pivotal verse. The various concepts represented by each of these words converge in one sentence, directing all the related themes to a single focal point. The numerical symmetry acts like a web that binds word to word, and theme to theme.

The first example of numerical convergence occurs in the last verse of the very first chapter of Genesis:

> And God *saw* *all* that He had *made*, and, behold, it was very *good*.
>
> (1:31)

made עשה
1:7, 11, 12, 16, 25, 26, 31

all כל
1:21, 21, 25, 26, 26, 28, 29, 29, 29, 30, 30, 30, 30, 31

Four words make their seventh appearance in this verse. In addition to the *seventh saw* (וירא) and *seventh good* (טוב) enumerated above, the word *made* (עשה) is written here for the *seventh* time, and *all* (כל) for the *fourteenth* time. God looked at *all* the various details of the world He had *made* and declared them to be very *good*. This numerical convergence of *saw, all, made,* and *good,* in the last verse of Genesis 1, brings the six days of physical creation to completion.

When we include the word *that* (כי) in the expression *saw that it was good* (וירא ... כי־טוב), we come to a seventh that is the inverted completion of the first. The *first* time this expression is used is in relation to the spiritual light of creation:

> And God *saw* the light *that* [it was] *good*.   וירא אלקים את־האור כי־טוב
>
> (1:4)

The *seventh* recording of the expression *saw that* [something was] ... *good* is in Genesis 3:6:

> ותרא האשה כי טוב העץ למאכל....
>
> And when the woman *saw* the tree *that it was good* for eating. ...

What Eve perceives is a perversion of the *very good* world that God had made, the opposite of the spiritual of light creation.

In this pivotal verse, we find another remarkable example of numerical convergence: Every key word appears here for a *seventh* time, counting from the beginning of the Torah:

> And the woman **saw** the *tree* ***that it was good*** for *eating*, and that it was a delight to the eyes, and the ***tree*** was desirable to make one wise, she took from its ***fruit*** and she did *eat*, and she gave to her husband with her, and he did ***eat***. (3:6)

The word *tree* appears in this verse for the *fourteenth* time in the Torah, the root of the word *eat/food* (אכל), in its last recording in the verse, for the *fourteenth* time – *seven* within Chapter 3, *fruit* (as a noun) for the *seventh* time, and the expression *saw . . . that*[15] *it was good* (וירא . . . כי־טוב) for the *seventh* time.

What does this all mean? To uncover the secret of these numerical patterns we must explore the relationship between the *seventh* and the *first*.

Understanding the Seventh in Relation to the First

Within a given literary unit, key words in the Torah often appear in multiples of seven. When the Torah does this, she wants to emphasize the theme represented by these words, and to draw attention to the verses wherein each word lives. When we compare the context of the first occurrence to the seventh, a deeper understanding of the text emerges. The *seventh* is connected to the *first*, with the context of the *first* defining the essence of the word.

As we have just noted, the *seventh* time we find the words *tree* and *fruit* in the Torah is in the verse that describes Eve eating from the forbidden tree:

> And the woman saw the *tree* that it was good for *eating*, and that it was a delight to the eyes, and the ***tree*** was desirable to make one wise, so she took from its ***fruit*** and she did *eat*, and she gave to her husband with her, and he did *eat*. (Genesis 3:6)

Tree and *fruit* appear together in their *first* appearance, as well:

> And God said, "Let the earth sprout vegetation: seed-bearing plants, ***fruit trees*** of every kind on earth that bear *fruit* with the seed in it."

---

tree עץ
1:11, 12, 29, 29; 2:9, 9, 9, 16, 17; 3:1, 2, 3, 6, 6

eat/food אכל
1:29, 30; 2:9, 16, 16, 17, 17; 3:1, 2, 3, 5, 6, 6, 6

וירא . . . כי־טוב
saw . . . that it was good
1:4, 10, 12, 18, 21, 25; 3:6

And it was so. The earth brought forth vegetation: seed-bearing plants of every kind, and *trees* of every kind bearing *fruit* with the seed in it. And God saw that this was good. (1:11–12)

The seventh appearance of *fruit* and *tree* is connected to the first. The numerical symmetry tells us not to forget that the *tree* and the *fruit* that Eve had come to desire was just one of the many *fruit trees* that God had created for the human being to enjoy. There were many trees in the garden that were created by God, but Eve forsook what was given and took what was proscribed. The *first* occurrence of *eat* (אכל) emphasizes this point, also:

Behold, I give you every herb bearing seed, which is upon the face of all the earth, and every *tree*, on which is the *fruit* of a *tree* bearing seed; to you it shall be *for **eating*** (לאכלה). (1:29)

God had given the human being all the *fruit trees* for *eating*. Adam and Eve *ate* from the one tree that God had set off limits.

Certainly, this is not a new idea, but this simple concept is reinforced by the numerical symmetry that connects the seventh *eat*, *tree*, and *fruit* to the first. *The Torah wants us to connect the seventh to the first to reveal an integrated theme.*

Searching for the Seventh

Sometimes, when we count a key word within a given section, we come up short of a multiple of seven. However, if we look a little further, we often find a seventh nearby, or sometimes in a text many chapters later. It may be the Torah is using a larger literary unit for this word. A test to determine whether or not such a count is valid is that the context of the seventh should have an apparent connection to the context of the first.

For example, the word *created* (ברא) appears only *six* times in the account of Creation (Genesis 1:1–2:3). Given all that we have said, we would expect to find seven in the Creation narrative, but the *seventh* is not far off:

These are the generations of the *heaven* and the *earth* when they were *created* (בהבראם), in the day the LORD God made *earth* and *heaven*. (2:4)

And the *seventh* reflects the *first*:

> In the beginning *God created* (ברא) the *heaven* and the *earth*. (1:1)

In both instances, *create* appears together with the words *heaven*, *earth*, and *God*. By connecting the seventh *created* to the first, the Torah is telling us to treat the two accounts of Creation as one.[16] The history of heaven and earth flashes back to the details of the creation of man on Day Six.

* * *

Let us examine another example. The word *dream* (חלום) is prominent in the story of the selling of Joseph (Genesis 37). *Dream* occurs there thirteen times. We might have expected to find fourteen, but upon further investigation, we do find a multiple of seven. If we look at the Joseph story as a whole, the word *dream* appears a total of *forty-two* times, that is, six times seven. The *first* occurrence of the word *dream* in the Joseph story reads:

> And *Joseph dreamed* a *dream* (ויחלם יוסף חלום), and he told it to his brothers; and they hated him all the more. (37:5)

The *forty-second* is a recollection of the *first*:

> ויזכר יוסף את החלמות אשר חלם
> And *Joseph* remembered the *dreams* that he had *dreamt* . . . . (42:9)

The Torah uses the numerical symmetry of words to identify literary units of different sizes, often overlapping like concentric circles. In this case, *dream* does not appear for a multiple of seven times in Genesis 37 in order to suggest that the dream theme is not yet complete. It extends throughout the narrative of Joseph and his brothers, where it recurs *forty-two* times altogether, culminating when the first dream reaches consummation at the end. Both the *first* and the *forty-second* have a doubling of the word *dream* with *Joseph* as the subject.

dream   חלום
37:5, 5, 6, 6, 8, 9, 9,
9, 9, 10, 10, 19, 20;
40:5, 5, 5, 5, 8, 8,
9, 9, 16; 41:1, 5, 7,
8, 11, 11, 11, 11, 12,
12, 15, 15, 15, 17, 22,
25, 26, 32; 42:9, 9

Series of Seven to Identify Units of Perfection

Seven is a number of perfection. The Seventh Day completes and perfects the six days of Creation, infusing holiness and blessing into the physical world: *And God blessed the seventh day to make it holy* (Genesis 2:3). As such, God blesses the Patriarchs with a blessing that contains *seven* expressions of benison, each predicate verb making one blessing (Cassuto).

God blesses Abram:
1. And I will make of you a great nation,
2. and I will bless you,
3. and I will make your name great,
4. so that you shall be a blessing.
5. I will bless those who bless you,
6. and he who curses you I will curse;
7. and through you will all the families of the earth be blessed.

(12:2–3)

Similarly, Isaac receives a *sevenfold* blessing:
1. and I will be with you,
2. and I will bless you;
3. for to you, and to your seed, I will give all these lands,
4. and I will perform the oath which I swore to Abraham your father:
5. And I will make your seed multiply as the stars of heaven,
6. and I will give to your seed all these lands;
7. and in your seed shall all the nations of the earth be blessed.

(26:3–4)

Again, we find a *sevenfold* blessing given to Jacob:
1. Therefore, may God give you of the dew of heaven, and the fatness of the earth, and plenty of grain and wine.
2. Let people serve you,
3. and nations bow down to you.
4. Be lord over your brothers,
5. and let your mother's sons bow down to you.
6. Cursed be they who curse you,
7. and blessed be they who bless you.

(27:28–29)

All of these blessings, governed by seven predicate verbs each, end in the universal theme that all peoples of the earth will receive blessings through the Patriarchs:

To Abram: *through you shall all the families of the earth be blessed.*
To Isaac: *through your seed shall all the nations of the earth be blessed.*
To Jacob: *blessed be they who bless you.*

Chapter 4

Numerical Symmetry as a Unifying Factor within Literary Units

BIBLICAL CRITICS HAVE claimed that the Torah text is a composite work of different authors, and that a redactor (R) combined different documents into one, leaving in place repetitions, contradictions, and differences in style and ethics. Each author is said to have used different names of God, so that writer J used the Tetragrammaton, while writer E used *Elokim*. The redactor, it is claimed, put the documents side by side, or took strands from one and then another, creating a composite text, but he was careful not to change the actual words of the documents themselves because they were held sacred. As a result, duplications and contradictions were left in place.

If this documentary hypothesis were correct, then the number of times each word appears in a composite text would be random. However, within literary sections of text, we find a strong unifying numerical symmetry. Key words are frequently found within passages in multiples of seven, and these words express the theme of the section. We have already seen this phenomenon in the first chapter of Genesis. We saw that many of the words and phrases in Genesis 1 appear in multiples of seven: *God, earth, on the earth, day/days, bird/fly, creeps/creeping, swarms, all/every,* and *God saw . . . good.* Within the seven paragraphs of the section, one for each day, key words are found seven times: *water* in Days Two and Three, *light* in Day Four, and *after its kind* in Days Four and Five. In addition, we found patterns of seven in the number of words and in the number of letters throughout the Creation narrative.

It is not that surprising that sevens would be emphasized in the account of the seven days of creation. Does the phenomenon of pivotal words occurring in multiples of seven persist beyond the Creation narrative? A few more examples taken from the next few sections of Genesis will serve to illustrate how tightly each section of the Torah is bound. Not only do we find this pattern within small literary units, say the size of a chapter, but the numerical pattern persists across larger units of text, uniting many chapters, or even tying one book of the Pentateuch to another. Indeed, some key words, like the names of the Patriarchs and the four-letter name of God, have symmetries that bind the entire Torah into an exquisite unity.

The Garden of Eden (Genesis 2:4–3:24)

In the story of the Garden of Eden, numerical symmetry based on the number seven persists.

Field (שדה) appears *seven* times in the section. These are the first seven occurrences of *field* in the Torah.

The verb *make/do* (עשה) occurs *seven* times.

The word *life/beast* (חי/חיה) is written *fourteen* times.

All (כל) is found *seven* times in Chapter 3.

Man/woman (איש/אשה) totals *twenty-one* times in section.

The words *man* (אדם) and *ground* (אדמה) have the same root, for *man* comes from the dust of the *ground*. These words total *thirty-five*, counting from the beginning of the Torah to the end of the narrative about Man in the Garden of Eden. In chapter 2 of this section, where *man* is formed from the dust of the *ground*, these words total *twenty-one*.

* * *

In all the key words that recur in multiples of seven in the Garden of Eden story, the *seventh* is related to the *first*.

For example, the *first* occurrence of *field* (שדה) in the Torah points to the *seventh*, forcing us to consider the interrelationship between these two verses.

---

field שדה
Genesis 2:5, 5, 19, 20; 3:1, 14, 18

make/do עשה
2:4, 18; 3:1, 7, 13, 14, 21

life/beast חי/חיה
2:7, 7, 9, 19, 19, 20; 3:1, 14, 14, 17, 20, 22, 22, 24

all כל
3:1, 1, 14, 14, 14, 17, 20

man/woman איש/אשה
2:22, 23, 23, 24, 24, 25; 3:1, 2, 4, 6, 6, 8, 12, 13, 13, 13, 15, 16, 17, 20, 21

man אדם
1:26, 27; 2:5, 7, 7, 8, 15, 16, 18, 19, 19, 20, 20, 21, 22, 22, 23, 25; 3:8, 9, 12, 17, 20, 21, 22, 24

ground אדמה
1:25; 2:5, 6, 7, 9, 19; 3:17, 19, 23

First: All thorns of the *field* were not yet on the earth, and all grain of the field had not yet sprouted, for the LORD God had not sent rain upon the earth and there was no man to till the ground. (2:5)

Seventh: Thorns and thistles shall it sprout for you, and you shall eat the grain of the *field*. By the sweat of your brow shall you eat bread ... (3:18)

The plants that had not yet sprouted in Genesis 2 were the plants of the cultivated field – the grain planted by man, and the thorns that would make his work in the field difficult,[17] as the next verse continues, "By the sweat of your brow shall you eat bread" (3:19). The *first* appearance of *field* in the Torah foreshadows the *seventh*, where it is written that man must labor in the *field* in order to eat bread.

* * *

made עשה
2:4, 18; 3:1, 7, 13, 14, 21

There is a sevenfold unit for the word *made* in the story of the Garden of Eden. The transcendent God who *made* earth and heaven is the same loving God who made garments for Adam and Eve.

First: ... in the day that the LORD God *made* earth and heaven. (2:4)

Seventh: And the LORD God *made* for Adam and his wife garments of skin, and He clothed them. (3:21)

The message of this word unit is that the awesome Creator of heaven and earth is concerned with the mundane needs of the human being. The making of a simple garment to clothe the naked is as weighty as the making of heaven and earth.

* * *

The word *all/every* (כל) flows in many cycles of seven in the Book of Genesis. In Genesis 1, the Torah speaks of *all* the living creatures in the sea, in the air, and on land. At the fourteenth appearance of *all* (כל), in the last verse of chapter one, God looks upon *all* that He had made and declares it to be very good.

In Genesis 3, *all* appears *seven* times:

First: The serpent was more cunning than *all* the beasts of the field that the
LORD God had made. (3:1)

Seventh: The man called his wife's name Eve, because she had become the
mother of *all* living. (3:21)

Eve is the mother of all mankind, but here, at the *seventh all* in the chapter,
she is called "the mother of *all living*," forming a nexus with the *first all* –
the serpent who was "more cunning than *all* the beasts of the field." The
external evil inclination had become internal. The cunning of the serpent
now resided *within* the human being. Eve is the mother of *all*, of both the
animal and spiritual inclinations. Her name means *life*, and life within the
human being includes the *all* of the serpent, who is "more cunning than
all the beasts," and the holy *all* of God, Who, at the twice seventh *all* in the
Torah, "saw *all* that He had made, and behold, it was very good."

* * *

The word *life/beast* (חי/חיה) occurs *fourteen* times in the section. Man is
given a Godly soul, a *neshama of life,* but because of his sin, he is banished
from the Tree of Life. However, there is a path back to the Tree of Life
guarded by the *cherubim*.

life/beast חי/חיה
2:7, 7, 9, 19, 19, 20;
3:1, 14, 14, 17, 20,
22, 22, 24

First: And the LORD God formed the man of dust from the ground, and
He blew into his nostrils the soul of *life*; and man became a *living* soul.
(2:7)

Fourteenth: He drove out the man and stationed at the east of the Garden
of Eden the *cherubim* and the flame of the ever-turning sword, to
guard the way to the Tree of *Life*. (3:24)

The soul of man is nourished by Torah, which is called "a *tree of life*" (Proverbs 3:18). The Torah is kept by the *cherubim*, which lie upon the ark cover:

It is there that I will set My meetings with you, and I shall speak with
you from atop the ark cover, from between the two *cherubim* that are

on the ark of the testimonial tablets, everything that I shall command you to the Children of Israel. (Exodus 25:22)

It is the *cherubim* that guard the way back to the Tree of Life in the Garden (Genesis 3:24). The relationship of the first to this seventh teaches that Man was created as a living soul to partake of the Tree of *Life* – the Torah.

* * *

The word *bread* (לחם) appears for the *first* time in the Torah in the Garden of Eden narrative:

First in Torah: By the sweat of your face shall you eat **bread**. ...
(Genesis 3:19)

bread לחם
Genesis 3:19; 14:18; 18:5; 21:14; 25:34; 27:17; 28:20; 31:54, 54; 35:19; 37:25; 39:6; 41:54, 55; 43:25, 31, 32; 45:23; 47:12, 13, 15, 17, 17,19; 48:7; 49:20; Exodus 2:20; 16:3, 4, 8, 12, 15, 22, 29, 32

In Exodus 16, in the story of the manna, *bread* appears eight times, the first of which marks the *twenty-eighth* time in the Torah (4 × 7th), and the last of which marks the *thirty-fifth* time (5 × 7th).

Twenty-eighth in Torah: The Israelites said to them, "If only we had died by the hand of the LORD in the land of Egypt, when we sat by the flesh pots, when we ate our fill of **bread**. For you have brought us out into this wilderness to starve this whole congregation to death."
(Exodus 16:3)

Twenty-ninth in Torah (first of the last seven): And the LORD said to Moses, "I will *rain* down **bread** for you from the sky, and the people shall go out and gather each day that day's portion — that I may thus test them, to see whether they will follow My Torah or not." (16:4)

Thirty-fifth in Torah (seventh from Exodus 16:4): Moses said: "This is the word that the LORD has commanded: 'An *omer* of it for safekeeping throughout your generations, in order that they may see the **bread** that I had you eat in the wilderness when I brought you out of the land of Egypt.'" (16:32)

The numerical symmetry of the first and seventh suggests a connection between Genesis 3:19 and Exodus 16:32. The curse of *by the sweat of your brow shall you eat bread* was lifted for the generation of the wilderness. In the Garden, there was *no grain of the field* and *God had not caused it to rain* (המטיר) because *there was no man to till the ground*, but in the Sinai desert, God had *caused it to rain* (ממטיר) *bread from the heavens*. In Eden, the LORD God had given one command, not to eat from the Tree of the Knowledge of Good and Evil. As Israel approached Mount Sinai, God gave them one command, not to gather manna on the Seventh Day. In Eden, Man was banished from the Tree of Life that lies in the *midst of the Garden*, but at Sinai, Moses would enter into the *midst of the cloud*, and Israel would receive the Torah, which is called "a *tree of life*."[18] In many ways, Israel's forty-year sojourn in the wilderness was a return to the condition of food-without-work that had once been Man's in Eden.

In the Garden of Eden narrative, symmetries of seven are formed with the words *field, man/ground, make/do, life, all,* and *bread*. These words are central to the major themes of the text – the *making* of earth and heaven, serpent, garments, and woman; the formation of *Man* from the dust of the *ground*; the sin that they *did*; *life*, as in the Tree of *Life*, animal *life*, and the mother of *all living*; and *field*, the domain of the snake, and the place where man is to labor for his *bread*.

Cain and Abel (Genesis 4)

In the Cain and Abel narrative (Genesis 4:1–17),[19] we find sevenfold repetitions of the key words *Cain, Abel,* and *brother*:

> *Abel* (הבל) appears *seven* times.
> *Cain* (קין) occurs twice *seven* times[20].
> *Brother* (אח) is written *seven* times.

In the first and seventh *Abel* in this narrative, we find an emphasis on his sibling relationship:

First: Then she bore his *brother Abel*. (4:2)

Seventh: Where is *Abel* your *brother*? (4:9)

Abel	הבל
4:2, 2, 4, 4, 8, 8, 9	
Cain	קין
4:1, 2, 3, 5, 5, 6, 8,	
8, 9, 13, 15, 15, 16, 17	
brother	אח
4:2, 8, 8, 9, 9, 10, 11	

The theme of sibling rivalry is emphasized by the numerical symmetry of the protagonists and their fraternal relationship. As we shall see, this theme, and the numerical symmetry that binds it, continues throughout the Book of Genesis.

* * *

Cain's birth is associated with God's Name, but in the end, he leaves the presence of the LORD and starts a new family in exile. The movement away from God is emphasized by the numerical symmetry of *Cain,* from his own birth to the birth of his son.

First Cain: And Adam *knew* (ידע) Eve, *his wife* (את אשתו), *and she conceived* (ותהר) *and bore* (ותלד) **Cain**, saying, I have acquired a man *with the* LORD (יהוה־).   (4:1)

Fourteenth Cain: Cain *left the presence of the* LORD (יהוה־) and settled in the land of Nod, east of Eden. *And* **Cain** *knew* (וידע) *his wife* (את־ אשתו), and *she conceived* (ותהר) *and bore* (ותלד) Enoch.   (4:16–17)

The numerical symmetry of *Cain,* forms a bracket that moves from "with the LORD" to "left the presence of the LORD." In both the *first* and the *fourteenth,* we find the phrases, *and he knew his wife, and she bore, and she conceived.* Eve associates the conception of her firstborn with God, but for Cain's firstborn, there is no such association. Rather, Cain has *left the presence of the* LORD. By comparing the first to the seventh, we observe the contrast between Cain's conception and that of his first child. There is a negative movement from the birth of Cain to the birth of Enoch.

In addition, note the following pattern of sevens in Genesis 4:

The first verse of the Cain and Abel narrative has *fourteen* words, and *forty-nine* letters (7×7).

The generations of Cain number *seven.*

giving birth ילד
4:17, 18, 18, 18, 18,
20, 22

The verb for *giving birth* (ילד) occurs *seven* times in the listing of Cain's descendants.

In the last verse of the account of the generations of Cain, the word *seven* is emphasized three times:

If Cain shall be avenged *sevenfold*,   כי שבעתים יקם־קין

then Lamech *seventy* and *sevenfold*.   ולמך שבעים ושבעה

(4:24)

This verse has *seven* words. The letters total *twenty-eight,* and they are divided by the cantillation marks into two groups of *fourteen,* twice *seven* each.

The writing style of sevens permeates the entire Torah, providing cogent evidence for single authorship.

The Combined Sections of Creation, the Garden of Eden, and Cain and Abel (Genesis 1–4)

The Creation narrative (Genesis 1–2:3) is connected to the section that follows by the numerical symmetry of the word *creation* (ברא). *Created* appears only six times in Genesis 1–2:3. The seventh is in the first verse of the next section, joining the first verse of Creation to the story of man in the Garden of Eden:

creation ברא
1:1, 21, 27, 27, 27;
2:3

First: In the beginning God *created* (ברא) the heavens and the earth. (1:1)

Seventh: These are the generations of the heavens and the earth, when they were *created* (בהבראם). . . . (2:4)

Created appears three more times, all hearkening back to the creation of Man:

This is the book of the generations of Adam. On the day that God *created* Adam, He made him in the likeness of God. He *created* them male and female. He blessed them and called their name Adam on the day they were *created.* (5:1–2)

Altogether, we find *created* ten times in the first five chapters of Genesis. These ten correspond to the ten statements of Creation in Genesis 1, where the phrase, *and God said,* is written ten times.

* * *

Adam/man אדם
1:26, 27; 2:5, 7, 7,
8, 15, 16, 18, 19, 19,
20, 20, 21, 22, 22,
23, 25; 3:8, 9, 12,
17, 20, 21, 22, 24;
4:1, 25

In the combined sections of Creation, the Garden of Eden and the first human family, we find numerical symmetry based on the number seven for *Adam/Man* (אדם), and for the various names of *God*.

Adam/Man (אדם), who is made in the image of God, appears in the combined sections *twenty-eight* times:. The four times seventh is a continuation of the human race. This verse is also the last time (the 40th) that אלקים, *God*, appears in these sections:

> And *Adam* (אדם) knew his wife again; and she bore a son, and called his name Seth, for "*God* has appointed me another seed instead of Abel, whom Cain slew."
>
> (4:25)

* * *

Ground אדמה
2:5, 6, 7, 9, 19; 3:17,
19, 23; 4:2, 3, 10,
11, 12, 14

Ground (אדמה) recurs *fourteen* times.

First: All thorns of the *field* were not yet on the earth, and all grain of the field had not yet sprouted, for the LORD God had not sent rain upon the earth and there was no man/*adam* (אדם) to *till the ground/adamah* (האדמה).
(2:5)

Fourteenth: Then He said, "What have you done? Behold, your brother's blood cries out to Me from the *ground*. Therefore, you shall be more cursed than the *ground*, which opened its mouth to receive your brother's blood from your hand. If you *till the ground*, it shall no longer yield its strength to you. You shall become a ceaseless wanderer on earth." Cain said to the LORD, "My punishment is too great to bear. Since You have banished me this day *from the face of the ground* (מעל פני האדמה), and from Your face shall I be hid; and I shall be a fugitive and a vagabond in the earth. ...
(4:10–14)

There was no man to till the *ground*. The blood of Cain's slain brother cries out from the *ground*, and if Cain should till the *ground*, it will withhold its strength from him. At the *fourteenth*, Cain is banished from the face of the *ground*. Cain, the farmer son of Adam, who was to *till the ground* of the field, becomes banished from that very *ground*, and from the face of God. The sevenfold unit of *ground* circumscribes a unified theme, wherein the purpose of providential rain becomes thwarted: instead of benefiting from rain upon the earth, Cain is driven from the *ground*. He becomes distanced from the Lord, and his descendants are destined to perish in an inundation of water: "I will destroy man whom I have created *from the face of the ground, from man* (מעל פני האדמה מאדם), to beast. ... (6:7). (Note the word play in Hebrew for "the ground, from man – *ha'adamah, me'adam*," emphasizing the connection of *man* [*adam*] to the *ground* [*adamah*].)

Seth continues the image of God in man – "a son in his likeness after his image" (5:3), which parallels, "Let us make man in our image, after our likeness" (1:26).

The Divine Names

Only one Divine Name is written in the account of the seven days of creation. The Name אלקים, *God*, is inscribed there *thirty-five* times.

In the stories of the Garden of Eden, and Cain and Abel, the various Divine Names are written *thirty-five* times, also. Within this total of five times seven, we find an inner symmetry based on two groupings of *half of ten, ten,* and *twice ten*:

God, אלקים, is written by itself *five* times, making a total of *forty* in Genesis 1–4).

Lord (יי׳הוה), by itself, appears *ten* times.

The combined Name, the *Lord God* (יי׳הוה אלקים), recurs *twenty* times.

The total for all the various Divine Names in the combined sections of Creation, the Garden of Eden, and Cain and Abel is *seventy*, a multiple of both *ten* and *seven*. At precisely the *seventieth* appearance of a Name of God, it is declared:

Then men began to call upon the name of the Lord. (4:26)

If we separate the compound name, *Lord God* (יי׳הוה אלקים), and count each of the names separately, *Lord* (יי׳הוה) and *God* (אלקים), we can discern numerical symmetry based on the number *six*. In the entire pericope, we find *God* (אלקים) *sixty* times, *ten* times *six*, a perfect sexagesimal number, and *Lord* (יי׳הוה) *thirty* times, five times *six*.

In the combined sections, the names of God incorporate numerical symmetry based on the numbers *seven, ten,* and *six*.

God   אלקים
1:1, 2, 3, 4, 4, 5, 6,
7, 8, 9, 10, 10, 11, 12,
14, 16, 17, 18, 20,
21, 21, 22, 24, 25,
25, 26, 27, 27, 28,
28, 29, 31; 2:2, 3, 3

God   אלקים
3:1, 3, 5, 5; 4:25

Lord   יהוה
4:1, 3, 4, 6, 9, 13,
15, 15, 16, 26

יהוה אלקים
Lord God
2:4, 5, 7, 8, 9, 15,
16, 18, 19, 21, 22;
3:1, 8, 8, 9, 13, 14,
21, 22, 23

Biblical critics assign these sections to different documents based upon the change of Divine Names, beginning at Genesis 2:4. However, the numerical symmetry of the Names of God, as well as the other repetition patterns we have noted, provide convincing proof of the unity of the Creation, Garden of Eden, and Cain and Abel narratives. This unity has its own message. God created a world that was *very good,* but the sins of Man brought evil into the world. The perfect world of God's creation, and the imperfect world brought about by the sins of Man are not two separate entities. It is one world – ours to destroy or perfect. But it is always God's world, and He places His token in the seventyfold frequency of His Names throughout the three sections.

man אדם
5:1, 1, 2, 3, 4, 5; 6:1,
2, 3, 4, 5, 6, 7, 7

אלקים
God/rulers
5:1, 1, 22, 24, 24;
6:2, 4

year שנה
5:3, 4, 5, 5, 6, 6, 7,
7, 8, 8, 9, 10, 10, 11,
11, 12, 13, 13, 14, 14,
15, 15, 16, 16, 17, 17,
18, 18, 19, 20, 20,
21, 22, 23, 23, 25,
25, 26, 26, 27, 27,
28, 28, 30, 30, 31,
31, 32; 6:3

day יום
5:1, 2, 4, 5, 8, 11, 14,
17, 20, 23, 27, 31;
6:3, 4

begat ילד
(Cain and Abel
to end of *Para-
shat Bereishit*)
4:1, 2, 17, 18, 18, 18,
18, 20, 22, 23, 25,
26; 5:3, 4, 4, 6, 7,
7, 9, 10, 10, 12, 13,
13, 15, 16, 16, 18, 19,
19, 21, 22, 22, 25,
26, 26, 28, 30, 30,
32; 6:1, 4

The Generations of Adam (Genesis 5:1–6:8)

In the section of the generations of Adam (Genesis 5:1–6:8), *Man* and *God* appear again in multiples of seven. *Man* (אדם) occurs *fourteen* times. *God/rulers* (אלקים) is written *seven* times.

We find the word *year* (שנה), which is used frequently in the section in reference to the various years of lives of the generations of Adam, a total of *forty-nine* times, *seven* times *seven.*

The word *day* recurs *fourteen* times.

In Chapter 5, which lists the generations from Adam to Noah, begat (ילד) appears *twenty-eight* times. In the combined sections from Cain and Abel to the end of the *parashah* (4:1–6:8), expressions for *giving birth* (ילד) total *forty-two.*

Words for *creation/making* total *seven*: *created* (ברא) four times (5:1, 2, 3; 6:7); and *made* (עשה) three times (5:1; 6:6, 7). These words appear together in two segments, forming a single unit:

> This is the book of the generations of Man. In the day God ***created*** Man, in the image of God ***made*** He him. Male and female ***created*** He them; and He blessed them, and called their name Adam, in the day when they were ***created***. (5:1–2)

> And the Lord regretted that He had ***made*** man on the earth, and it pained his heart. And the Lord said, "I will blot out Man whom

I have **created** from the face of the ground – from man to animal, to creeping things, and to birds of the sky; for I am regret that I **made** them."   (6:6–7)

In these sentences the words *made* and *created* are used interchangeably, totaling *seven* times altogether. The numerical symmetry binds these passages together, and the juxtaposition is startling. The creation of Man, who is made in God's image, is about to be undone. The world that God had *created* and the life that He had *made* was about to be destroyed.

This section lists the ten generations from Adam to Noah. It begins with the noble declaration of the creation of Man in the likeness of God (5:1–2), and ends with the announcement of the destruction of mankind and all life (6:6–7). By noting the movement from the first to the seventh in each of these sevenfold multiples, we observe the progressive degeneration of man on earth, from his once exalted state at the time of his creation to the degenerated level of the generation of the Flood.

Man, God, created/made, and *day* appear together in elevated tone in the opening verse of the section of the generations of Adam: "in the **day God created Man**, in the likeness of God **made** He him" (5:1). All these words are found at the end of the section, where they complete a sevenfold symmetry of multiples. In addition, the word *birth/begot* appears in the last paragraph of the section for the *forty-second* time in the Torah. The word *years* is written for the *forty-ninth* time in the section, beginning with, "When Adam had lived one hundred and thirty **years**, he begot in his likeness and his image . . ." (5:3). The image of God in man is passed on to Adam's son. By the *forty-ninth* appearance of the word *years* in the section (6:3), the image of God is desecrated by man's many sins, and his remaining *years* are numbered:

And the L ord said, "My spirit shall not abide in Man forever, since he is but flesh; his days shall be a hundred and twenty **years** [7 × 7th]." The *Nephilim* were on the earth in those **days** [2 × 7th] – and also afterward, when the sons of **god/rulers** [7th for *Elokim*] would consort with the daughters of man, who would **bear** [6 × 7th in the Torah] to them.[21] They were the mighty of old, men of name. The L ord saw that the wickedness of Man was great upon the earth, and that every product of the thoughts of his heart was but evil always.

And the LORD regretted that He had made Man on earth, and it
pained His heart. And the LORD said, "I will blot out **Man** whom
I have **created** from the face of the earth – from **Man** [2 × 7th] to
animal, to creeping things, and to birds of the sky; for I regret that I
made them [7th for *created/made*]." But Noah found grace in the eyes
of the LORD.   (6:3–8)

The beginning and end of the section contain many words that appear in
multiples of seven, all of which are found in the last paragraph quoted above.
The numerical symmetry in this section binds these words in a downward
progression. The generations of Adam are listed one after another, one *birth*
following another, with the length of *years* listed for each – *years* and *birth* in
multiples of seven. *Adam/Man*, is written *fourteen* times, moving from his
exalted creation to the decree of his destruction. The *day* that God creates
Man in the Divine image, in its *fourteenth* appearance of *day*, degenerates
to the *days* when the *Nephilim* are upon the earth who cohabit with the
daughters of men. What was *created* and *made* becomes a cause of regret
to the LORD. Even the Name used for all of creation, *Elokim*, is usurped by
the rulers who consort with the daughters of men. The *seventh* becomes an
inversion of the *first*.

However, within the spiraling degeneration of the progeny of Adam lay
the seed of regeneration: *But Noah found favor in the eyes of* the LORD (6:8).

Parashat Noah

Contrary to the view that the account of the Flood is a composite composi-
tion, the numerical symmetry of this section suggests that a unified text lies
before us.[22] When we count words that appear in multiples of seven, we can
feel the pulse of their sevenfold rhythm as these words flow through the
body of an organic whole. The *first* introduces the theme of each word; the
seventh completes the motif.

Noah   נֹחַ
6:9, 9, 9, 10, 13, 22;
7:1, 5, 6, 7, 9, 9, 11,
13, 13, 13, 15, 23; 8:1,
6, 11, 13, 15, 18, 20;
9:1, 8, 17

THE FLOOD (GENESIS 6:9–9:17)

In the account of the Flood (Genesis 6:9–9:17), *Noah* appears *twenty-eight*
times.[23]

First: These are the generations of **Noah** – Noah was a wholly righteous man in his generations; Noah walked with *God*. (6:9)

Twenty-eighth: And *God* said to **Noah**, "This is the sign of the covenant . . . ." (9:17)

The *parashah* begins with Noah walking with God. At the twenty-eighth appearance of his name, Noah, the father of a renewed mankind, reaches the climax of his mission, as he receives the rainbow covenant.

When we include the prelude and the aftermath of the Flood, we find *Noah seven* more times, bringing the total to *thirty-five* in Genesis 6 through 9.

Noah   נח
6:8; 9:18, 19, 20,
24, 28, 29

First: But **Noah** found favor in the eyes of the LORD. (6:8)

Thirty-fifth: And all the days of **Noah** were nine hundred and fifty years: and he died. (9:29)

This count links the last verse of *Parashat Bereishit* to the end of **Noah's** life.

* * *

The root of *destroy* (שחת), which is found near the beginning and the end of the section, occurs *seven* times.

destroy   שחת
6:11, 12, 12, 13, 17;
9:11, 15

First: Now the earth had become ***destructive*** before God; and the earth had become filled with violence. (6:11)

Seventh: I will remember My covenant between Me and you and every living being among all flesh, and the water shall never again become a flood to ***destroy*** all flesh. (9:15)

The *destructive* behavior of the generation of the Flood led to the *destruction* of the earth and all life, save those in the ark. The *seventh* appearance of the word, *destroy*, marks God's promise never again to *destroy* all life by flood. God places a limit on His attribute of Justice, tempering it with His attribute of loving-kindness.

* * *

God speaks to Noah *seven* times (6:13; 7:1; 8:15; 9:1, 8, 12, 17).

First: *God said to Noah*, "The end of *all flesh* has come before Me, for the *earth* is filled with violence through them; and behold, I am about to destroy them from the *earth*." (6:13)

Seventh: *God said unto Noah*, "This is the sign of the covenant, which I have established between me and *all flesh* that is on the *earth*." (9:17)

By the seventh time God speaks to Noah, the message of an *end to all flesh* on the *earth* becomes transposed into the protective *covenant between God and all flesh* on the *earth*. In the first and seventh theophany, we find a repetition of six words: *God, said, Noah, all, flesh,* and *earth*. The seventh Divine communication marks a completion of the first.

flesh בשר
6:12, 13, 17, 19;
7:15, 16, 21; 8:17;
9:4, 11, 15, 15, 16, 17

* * *

Flesh (בשׂר) appears *fourteen* times.

First: And *God* saw the earth and behold it was destructive, for *all flesh* had destructed its way *upon the earth*. (6:12)

Fourteenth: And *God* said to Noah, "This is the sign of the covenant that I have established between Me and *all flesh* that is *upon the earth*." (9:17)

After the Flood, the covenant *of the rainbow* tempered *God's* attribute of strict judgment so that *all flesh upon the earth* would no longer be subject to destruction due to the destructive behavior of Man. The numerical symmetry of the word *flesh*, together with the shared phrase, *all flesh . . . upon the earth*, reinforces this interconnection.

make עשה
6:14, 14, 15, 16, 16,
22, 22

ark תבה
6:14, 14, 15, 16, 16,
18, 19

* * *

The words *make* (עשׂה) and *ark* (תבה) are found together for the first time in the *parashah* in Genesis 6. Both words appear *seven* times in the chapter, in the paragraph that deals with the *making* of the *ark*.

First: *Make* for yourself an **ark** of gopher wood; make it an ark with compartments, and cover it inside and out with pitch. (6:14)

Seventh: And from all that lives, of all flesh, two of each shall you bring into the **ark** to keep alive with you ... And Noah made according to everything God had commanded him, so did he *make*. (6:19–22)

The command to *make an ark* reaches completion at the level of the seventh, when the purpose of the ark is revealed – *to keep all flesh alive*. The sevenfold symmetry of *make* and *ark* binds this paragraph together.

* * *

למינה
after its kind
6:20, 20, 20; 7:14,
14, 14, 14

After their/its kind (למינה/למינהו) recurs *seven* times in the Noah narratives.

First: From birds **after their kind**, and from the cattle **after its kind**, and from all creeping things of the ground **after their kind**, two of each shall come to you to keep alive. (6:20)

Seventh: ... they and every beast **after its kind**, all the cattle **after its kind**, every creeping thing that creeps on the earth **after their kind**, and every winged creature **after their kind**, every bird, every wing: they came to Noah into the ark.... (7:14–15)

All seven fall within two verses that depict the entire diversity of animal life upon the land – the first three regarding the animals that are to come into the ark, and the last four in relation to their actual entry into the ark.

* * *

come   בא
7:1, 7, 9, 13, 15, 16,
16

The word *come/came/enter* (בא) is found *seven* times in Chapter 7, all in the paragraphs related to *entering* the ark.

First: Then the LORD said to Noah, "**Come**, you and all your household into the ark, for it is you that I have seen to be righteous before Me in this generation." (7:1)

Seventh: Those that *came*, male and female of all flesh they came, as God had commanded him. And the LORD shut him in. (7:16)

God commands Noah and his household to *enter* the ark. The word בא (*come/came/enter*) becomes complete at its seventh appearance, when the LORD shuts in all the animals that have *entered* the ark.

* * *

Water is found twenty-one times in the section. For details, see next section on *Parashat Noah* as a whole.

* * *

flood מבול
6:17; 7:6, 7, 10, 17; 9:11, 11, 15, 28; 10:1, 32; 11:10

We would expect the word *flood* (מבול) to occur seven times in the section, but we find *flood* only *twelve* times in *Parashat Noah*. The sexagesimal system, based upon sixes and twelves, represents the physical creation that God made in six days. This number is emphasized in the 120 years God granted Man before the deluge, and the 600 years of Noah at the time of the Flood.

* * *

covenant ברית
9:9, 11, 12, 13, 15, 16, 17

In Chapter 9, which deals with the covenant between God and Noah, the word *covenant* (ברית) appears *seven* times.[24]

First: I now *establish* My **covenant** with you and your offspring after you, and with every living thing that is with you – birds, cattle, and every wild beast as well – *all* that have come out of the ark, every living thing of *the earth*. (9:9–10)

Seventh: [The rainbow] shall be the sign of the **covenant** that I have *established* between Me and *all* flesh that is on *the earth*. (9:17)

The *seventh* is a reflection of the *first*, each verse sharing the words *establish*, *covenant*, *all*, and *the earth*.

A Series of Firsts

The main idea of the Flood story becomes apparent when we read the verses containing the *first* appearance of each word or phrase, cited in the pages above:

Divine beings saw the daughters of men that they were fair; and they took themselves wives from **all** that they chose (6:2). These are the offspring of **Noah** – Noah was a righteous man, wholehearted in his generation; Noah walked with God (6:9). . . . . Now the earth had become **destructive** before God; and the earth had become filled with robbery (6:11)....And God saw the earth and behold it was destructive, for all *flesh* had destructed its way upon the earth (6:12). **God said to Noah,** "The end of all flesh has come before Me, for the earth is filled with violence through them; and behold, I am about to destroy them from the earth (6:13). **Make** for yourself an **ark** of gopher wood. . . . (6:14). Behold, I am about to bring the **Flood** – **waters** upon the earth – to destroy all flesh in which there is a breath of life from under the heavens; everything that is in the earth shall die" (6:17). Then Hashem said to Noah, "**Come** to the ark, you and all your household, for it is you that I have seen to be righteous before Me in this generation (7:1). God remembered Noah and **all**[25] the beasts and all the animals that were with him in the ark, and God caused a wind to pass over the earth, and the waters subsided (8:1). I will confirm My **covenant** with you – Never again shall all flesh be cut off by the waters of the Flood, and never again shall there be a flood to destroy the earth" (9:11).

By following the verses wherein the *first* of these sevenfold expressions lie, we arrive at a full summary of the story. Many of these words are found clustered together for their "seventh" appearance at the end of the Flood narrative:

"I will remember My covenant between Me and you and every living being among all flesh, and the **water** shall never again become a flood to **destroy** all flesh. And the bow shall be in the cloud, and I will look upon it to remember the everlasting covenant between God and every living being among all flesh that is on earth." **And God said to Noah,** "This is the sign of the **covenant** that I have confirmed between Me and **all flesh** that is upon the earth." (9:15–17)

God's *seventh* and last *communication with Noah* was to confirm the *covenant* of the rainbow, never to *destroy all flesh* by *water*. The making of this covenant suggests that this pact was needed. In order for the saga of Man to continue, it was necessary for God to temper His attribute of justice. The message of the Flood may be that when God relates to Man through His attribute of strict justice, Man cannot endure, and the purpose of creation is thwarted. The rainbow covenant ensured that a nation would arise from a man, Abraham, who would walk before God. Noah's covenant made possible that human partners could survive error and grow to walk before God. This motif is supported by the sevenfold symmetry of each of the key words, uniting the section into a perfect whole.

When we take the words, which appear for the *first* time within a literary unit, and compare them to the *seventh*, we find each *seventh* is a completion of the *first*. Each of these words, within their overlapping literary units, has a life of its own, beginning with its birth, when the word emerges for the *first* time in the text, and climaxing at its *seventh*, or multiple thereof, when the word matures to a state of completion.

seven שבעה
7:2, 2, 3, 3, 4, 10, 11; 8:4, 4, 10, 12, 14; 11:21, 26

earth (ch. 7) ארץ
7:3, 4, 6, 10, 12, 14, 17, 17, 18, 19, 21, 21, 23, 24

earth (ch. 8–10)
8:1, 3, 7, 9, 11, 13, 14, 17, 17, 17, 19, 22; 9:1, 2, 7, 10, 10, 11, 13, 14, 16, 17, 18; 10:8, 10, 11, 25, 32

earth (ch. 11)
11:1, 2, 4, 8, 9, 9, 28

water מים
6:17; 7:6, 7, 10, 17, 18, 18, 19, 20, 24; 8:1, 3, 3, 5, 7, 8, 9, 11, 13; 9:11, 15

Parashat Noah as a Whole (Genesis 6:8–11:32)

When we examine *Parashat Noah* as a whole, including the generations of Noah and the Tower of Babel, we find, once more, numerical symmetry based upon the number *seven*.

The word *seven* (שבעה) is found *seven* times in Genesis 7, and *fourteen* times in the whole of *Parashat Noah*.

* * *

The exact form of the word earth, ארץ,[26] appears *fourteen* times in Chapter 7, *twenty-eight* times in Chapters 8 through 10, and *seven* times in chapter 11. In Chapters 7–11, the total for the word ארץ is *forty-nine*, *seven* times *seven*.

* * *

Water (מים) occurs *twenty-one* times in *Parashat Noah*. The *seventh* is connected to the *first*:

First: And as for Me – Behold, I am about to bring the *Flood* – **waters** upon the earth – *to destroy all flesh* in which there is a breath of life from under the heavens; *everything* that is in the earth shall expire. (6:17)

Seventh (× 3): I will remember My covenant between Me and you and
every living being among *all flesh,* and the **waters** shall never again
become a *flood to destroy all flesh.*   (9:15)

The *seventh* is a reversal of the *first.*

* * *

In the story of the Deluge, the words *flood* (מַבּוּל) and *rain* (גֶשֶׁם) are used
almost interchangeably: "And the *rain* was upon the earth forty days …."
(7:12); "And the *Flood* was forty days upon the earth …." (7:17). Together,
flood and *rain* total *fourteen* occurrences: *flood, twelve* times, a sexagesimal
number, and *rain,* two times.[27]

| **flood** | מבול |
| 6:17; 7:6, 7, 10, 17; |
| 9:11, 11, 15, 18; 10:1, |
| 32; 11:10 |

| **rain** | גשם |
| 7:12; 8:2 |

* * *

The Tetragrammaton,[28] the L ORD, appears *fourteen* times in *Parashat Noah*
– *seven* times in the story of Noah, and *seven* times in the story of Nimrod
and the tower of Babel. *Hashem* (the L ORD) reverses Nimrod's intent to
centralize humanity around the city of Babel:

| יהוה |
| L ORD (Noah) |
| 7:1, 5, 16; 8:20, 21, |
| 21; 9:26 |

First: He was a mighty hunter before **Hashem**; therefore it is said, *As
Nimrod the mighty hunter before Hashem.* And the beginning of his
kingdom was **Babel**. …   (10:9)

| יהוה |
| L ORD (Babel) |
| 10:9, 9; 11:5, 6, 8, |
| 9, 9 |

Seventh: Therefore is the name of it called **Babel**; because there did
Hashem confuse the language of all the earth; and from there did
Hashem scatter them across the face of all the earth.   (11:9)

Although the continuation of the genealogies interrupts the birth of Nimrod and the building of the tower of Babel, the symmetry of the name of the
L ORD unifies these sections.

* * *

HaAdam, mankind, appears *ten* times in the *parashah.* The world that was
created with *ten* utterances was to be destroyed because of the sins of Man.
If we begin the count a few verses before the beginning of *Parashat Noah,*
we can discern a unit of *fourteen* for *man,* where God informs us of His
intention to destroy that generation:

| **mankind** | האדם |
| 6:5, 6, 7, 7; 7:21, |
| 23; 8:21, 21; 9:5, 5, |
| 6, 6, 6; 11:5 |

First: And Hashem *saw* that the wickedness of **Man** was great upon the earth.... And Hashem said, "I will destroy *Man* whom I have created from *the face of the earth* ...." (6:5–7)

Twice Seventh: And the LORD came down to *see* the city and the tower, which the sons of **Man** have built ... So the LORD scattered them abroad from there upon *the face of all the earth.* (11:5–8)

The twice seventh completes the first and renews the cycle that began with the sins of *Man*. In both cases, Hashem *sees* the evil of *Man* and reacts – in the first instance by destroying *Man* from *the face of the earth,* and in the second instance by scattering *Man* across *the face of the earth.* This time, the response to the sins of man has been tempered by the rainbow covenant. God would not destroy mankind, but he would remain involved in their history.

* * *

Key words throughout the entire pericope of the Flood and its aftermath occur in multiples of seven: *Noah, Hashem, destroy, man, all, flesh, made, seven, come, water, rain/flood, covenant,* and the *seven Divine communications with Noah.* When we read this list slowly and recall the associations each word makes with the story of Noah, a complete recapitulation of the events comes to mind. The Torah uses word repetitions in numerical patterns to trace themes throughout the text.

Symmetries that Connect Parashat Noah to Other Parts of the Torah

ark   תבה
6:14, 14, 15, 16, 16, 18, 19; 7:1, 7, 9, 13, 15, 17, 18, 23; 8:1, 4, 6, 9, 9, 10, 13, 16, 19; 9:10, 18

Although the word *ark* (תבה) occurs *seven* times in Genesis 6, in the entire pericope, *ark* appears only twenty-six times, two short of a multiple of seven. However, there is another seventh, a seventh that is very much connected to the first. Ark (תבה) appears two more times in the Torah, in the story of Moses as an infant (Exodus 2:3, 5). The first two and last two of this sevenfold appearance of *ark* are very much related:

First two in the Torah: Make *for yourself* (לְךָ) an *ark of* (תבת) cedar wood, and pitch *the ark* (את־התבה) inside and outside with pitch.

(Genesis 6:14)

Twenty-seventh and twenty-eighth in the Torah: When she no longer could hide him, she took *for him* (לוֹ) an *ark of* (תבת) bulrushes, and daubed it with slime and with pitch ... and she [Pharaoh's daughter] saw *the ark* (את־התבה) among the reeds ... and she sent her hand-maid, and she fetched it. And she opened, and *she saw him* (ותראהו) *and behold* (והנה), a boy wept. And she had compassion on him, and she said, "One of the Hebrews' children is this."   (Exodus 2:3–6)

If we count the word *ark* backwards from this last appearance of *ark*, we find another unit of seven where the first is an echo of the seventh:

First of last unit of seven: and Noah removed the covering of *the ark* (התבה), *and he saw* (וירא), *and behold* (והנה), the face of the ground was dry.   (Genesis 8:13)

Noah was saved in an ark, and Moses was saved in an ark. "Noah *removed the covering* of the *ark*" and saw his salvation: "and he *saw, and behold,* the face of the ground was dry." The infant Moses's salvation came when Pharaoh's daughter *opened* the ark and discovered a baby: "and she *opened it* and she *saw* the child, and *behold,* a boy was weeping." God had compassion on Noah and the animals with him in the ark, and told him to leave the ark. Pharaoh's daughter had compassion on the Hebrew child and took him from the ark. Cassuto notes the parallels between the arks of Noah and Moses:

> In both cases there is to be saved from drowning one who is worthy of salvation and is destined to bring deliverance to others; here it is humanity that is to be saved, there the chosen people; here it is the macrocosm that has to be preserved, there it is the microcosm. The experiences of the fathers foreshadow the history of the descendants. Hence, similar expressions occur in both sections. . . .[29]

The sevenfold appearance of *ark*, along with the similar words and themes found in the first and the seventh, form a nexus between these seemingly disparate sections of the Torah. The *first ark* saves humanity; the second saves the man who would teach Torah to Israel and, by extension, to all humankind. The *first ark* preserves the physical body of Man; the *twenty-eighth ark* safeguards the human vehicle of spiritual revelation.

* * *

למינה
after its kind
6:20, 20, 20; 7:14,
14, 14, 14

In Genesis 1, *after its/their kind* (למינה/למינהו) appears *seven* times regarding animal life, and three more times in relation to plant life. In the Flood narrative, *after its/their kind* recurs *seven* more times. These are the only times *after its/their kind* appears in Genesis. The diversity of animal life reflected in the sevenfold use of forms of the word למינה in the Creation narrative is emphasized seven times regarding all the species brought into the ark. The Flood returns the earth to the water-world of Day One. The animals in the ark preserve the species that God had created during the first six days of the Beginning. The numerical symmetry of *after its/their kind* links the account of Creation to the renewal of Creation after the Flood.

* * *

עשב
herbage/grain
1:11, 12, 29, 30; 2:5;
3:18; 9:3

The word for *herbage/grain* (עשב) occurs *seven* times in the Book of Genesis. We encounter the *first* in Day Three of Creation:

> God said, "Let the earth sprout vegetation – **herbage** (עשב) yielding seed, fruit trees yielding fruit each after its kind, containing its own seed on the earth." And it was so. (1:11)

The *seventh* is found when God expands man's diet to include the eating of meat:

> Every moving thing that lives shall be food for you; like the green **herbage** (עשב), I have given you everything. (9:3)

After the Flood, God permits the eating of meat, but we are reminded that the herbage of Creation, the עשב, was all that God originally intended for Man's consumption. The numerical symmetry of the first and the seventh reinforces this theme.

* * *

The first seven times *night* is written in the Torah form a unit wherein the *seventh* reflects the *first*. Each of these seven appearances of *night* occurs together with the word *day*. The *first* is found at the beginning of Creation:

> And God called the light *day*, and the darkness He called **night**; and there was evening, and there was morning, one day.　　　(1:5)

The *seventh* occurs at the renewal of Creation at the end of the Flood:

> While the earth remains, seedtime and harvest, cold and heat, summer and winter, and *day* and **night** shall not cease.　　　(8:22)

Both verses have *forty-nine* Hebrew letters. The covenant made with Noah affirms the continuity of the natural order, symbolized by the *day* and *night* of Creation.

night ‏לילה‎
1:5, 14, 16, 18; 7:4, 12; 8:22

* * *

All/every (‏כל‎) is written *fourteen* times in the first chapter of the Torah. The *fourteenth all* also contains the *seventh* appearance of the expression *and God saw . . . good,* (‏וירא אלקים . . . טוב‎):

all/every ‏כל‎
1:21, 21, 25, 26, 26, 28, 29, 29, 29, 30, 30, 30, 30, 31

וירא אלקים את־כל אשר עשה והנה טוב מאד

And **God saw all** that he had made and, **behold**, it was very **good**. (1:31)

There are two parallels to this verse. The first takes place in the garden:

ותרא האשה כי טוב העץ . . . ותקח

And *the woman* **saw that** *the tree* **was good** . . . and she **took**. . . .　　　(3:6)

When we add the word ‏כי‎ (*that*), the verse above marks the *seventh* time the expression ‏וירא . . . כי טוב‎ – "and saw **that** [it] was good" – occurs in the Torah. The *seventh* is an inverse parallel of the *good* that God *saw* in creation. The second parallel occurs at the prelude to the Flood:

ויראו בני האלקים את־בנות האדם כי טבת הנה ויקחו להם נשים מכל אשר בחרו

The sons of **God/rulers saw** the daughters of men **that they** were **good**, and they took wives from **all** that they chose.　　　(6:2)

This verse is very similar in word and structure to the last verse of Creation quoted above. Both verses share the words *God/rulers, saw, good, all,* along with the play on the words *behold/they were* (הִנֵּה, הֵנָּה). Genesis 6:2 also shares words with the verse where Eve is tempted by the fruit of the tree (*and she saw that the tree was good*). Eve *sees* the tree as *good* to eat and she *takes*, and the sons of rulers *see* the daughters of men as *good*, and they *take* from *all* they desire. Both are perversions of the *good* that God beholds in *all* the stages of Creation. Both lead to catastrophe – the former to mortality and exile from Eden, the latter to inundation and death to *all* flesh. Both are a corruption of the *good that God saw* in *all that he had made*.

When we include the prelude to the Flood, counting from the beginning of Chapter 6, in verse 6:2 quoted above, through the end of the Flood narrative (9:17), we find the word *all* (כֹּל) *seventy* times: *fourteen* times in Chapter 6, *fourteen* times, in Chapter 8, and *forty-two* times, in the remainder of the pericope.

The prelude to the Flood began with the taking of wives from *all* that the sons of God/rulers had chosen. The words in this verse are a perversion of the last verse of Creation, where God sees *all that He had made to be very good*. By the *seventieth all*, counting from the beginning of Genesis 6, God promises never again to bring a flood to destroy the earth:

Seventieth: God said to Noah, "This is the sign of the covenant that I have established between me and ***all*** flesh that is upon the earth."   (9:17)

The symmetry of the word *all* moves from *all* the animals of creation (*fourteen* times in Chapter 1), to *all* the living things in Eden (*seven* times in Chapter 3), to ***all*** the animals saved on the ark (*seven* times in Chapter 8), to the covenantal promise never again to destroy *all* flesh upon the earth (*seventy* times in Chapter 6 through 9:17, the section of the Flood and its prelude). By following the symmetry of the word *all,* we survey the creation, destruction, and salvation of *all* life upon the earth.

To summarize this repetition pattern, when we count the number of times the word *all* (כֹּל) appears in each chapter, we find it *fourteen* times in Genesis 1, *seven* times in Chapter 3, *fourteen* times in Chapter 6, and *fourteen* times in chapter 8. Continuing beyond the Flood narrative, extending the count past Genesis 9:17 through the end of *Parashat Noah*, the word *all* turns up *twenty-one* times in the whole of Chapter 9, and *seven* times in

Chapter 11. As we shall see, the symmetry of this little word כֹּל continues into the next *parashah*.

all (ch. 11)   כֹּל

11:1, 4, 6, 6, 8, 9, 9

Nexus to Abram

THE NUMERICAL SYMMETRY OF THE WORD שֵׁם

The two-letter word שֵׁם can refer to Noah's son, *Shem* (שֵׁם), the word *name* (שֵׁם), or the word *there* (שָׁם), depending on the context. The word *name* (שֵׁם) identifies that which is over *there* (שָׁם), and the name of Noah's first son is simply, *Name* (שֵׁם). The numerical symmetry of this word forms a nexus to the next section, the story of Abraham.[30]

   Shem/name/there (שם) appears *seven* times in Genesis 10, the chronicle of Noah's descendants. The *seventh* is an echo of the *first*:

First, 10:1: These are the descendants of the sons of Noah – **Shem** (שֵׁם), Ham, and Japheth; sons were born to them after the Flood.

   10:14: . . . Pathrusim, and Casluhim, from **there** (מִשָּׁם) came forth the Philistines, and Caphtorim.

   10:21: Sons were also born to **Shem** (שֵׁם), ancestor of all the descendants of Eber and older brother of Japheth.

   10:22: The sons of **Shem** (שֵׁם): Elam, Asshur, Arpachshad, Lud, and Aram.

   10:25: Two sons were born to Eber: the **name** (שֵׁם) of the first was Peleg, for in his days the earth was divided; and the **name** (וְשֵׁם) of his brother was Joktan.

Seventh, 10:31: These are the descendants of **Shem** (שֵׁם) according to their clans and languages, by their lands, according to their nations.

The *seventh* echoes the *first*: "These are the descendants of the sons of Noah – **Shem**" (10:1); and, "These are the descendants of **Shem**" (10:31).

   Continuing our count into the next chapter, we find *name/there* (שם) *seven* times in the story of the Tower of Babel:

First, 11:2: And as they migrated from the east, they came upon a valley in the land of Shinar **and they settled there**. (וַיֵּשְׁבוּ שָׁם)

11:4: And they said, "Come, let us build for ourselves a city, and a tower with its top in the sky, and let us make for ourselves a **name** (שֵׁם) – *lest we shall be scattered all over the earth*."

11:7: Come-now, let us go down and let us baffle their language **there** (שָׁם), so that no man will understand the language of his neighbor.

11:8: Thus the LORD scattered them **from there** (מִשָּׁם) over the face of the whole earth; and they stopped building the city.

11:9: That is why **its name** (שְׁמָהּ) was called Babel, because **there** (שָׁם) the LORD confounded the speech of the whole earth;

Seventh, 11:9: **and from there** (וּמִשָּׁם) the LORD *scattered them* over the face of the whole earth.

God had told Noah to *fill the earth* (9:1), but they came upon a valley and decided to **settle there** (11:2), the first in a series of seven for the word **there/name**. But God's will was not to be thwarted, and by the seventh שׁם, the LORD had scattered them **from there** *over the face of the whole earth* (11:9). "They settled **there**" (וַיֵּשְׁבוּ שָׁם) was transformed into "He scattered them from **there**" (וּמִשָּׁם הֱפִיצָם) (11:2, 9).

In the remainder of Genesis 11, the word שׁם appears only *six* times, the last of which (11:31) reflects the beginning of the chapter (11:2), both containing the phrase, **and they settled there** (וַיֵּשְׁבוּ שָׁם). Terah, Abram's father, takes his family and *settles there* (וַיֵּשְׁבוּ שָׁם), but the LORD tells Abram to *go forth* (12:1).

First, 11:10: These are the descendants of **Shem** (שֵׁם). **Shem** (שֵׁם) was 100 years old when he begot[31] Arpachshad. . . .

11:11: After the birth of Arpachshad, **Shem** (שֵׁם) lived 500 years. . . .

11:29: Abram and Nahor took to themselves wives, the **name** (שֵׁם) of Abram's wife was Sarai, and the **name** (שֵׁם) of Nahor's wife was Milcah. . . .

11:31: Terah took his son Abram, his grandson Lot the son of Haran, and his daughter-in-law Sarai, the wife of his son Abram, and they set out together from Ur of the Chaldeans for the land of Canaan. And they came as far as Haran, ***and they settled there*** (וַיֵּשְׁבוּ שָׁם).

There are only six here, but the seventh שׁם is not far off. We find the seventh two verses later, in the blessing God gives to Abram at the start of the next *parashah*:

Seventh: The LORD said to Abram, "*Go forth* from your native land and from your father's house to the land that I will show you. I will make of you a great nation, and I will bless you; I will make ***your name*** (שְׁמֶךָ) great, and you shall be a blessing. I will bless those who bless you, and curse him that curses you; and all the families of the earth shall be blessed through you."   (12:1–3)

We have here a triple series of a sevenfold count of the word שׁם (*Shem/ there/name*), listing the descendants of Noah's sons, including *Shem*, their *names*, and the word *there*, referring to the places where they settled, built, and from where they were scattered. The sons of Noah generated the people of Babel, who had said, "Let us make for ourselves a ***name***" (נַעֲשֶׂה־לָּנוּ שֵׁם), but at the end of the third sevenfold series of שׁם, God tells Abram, "I will bless you, and I will make ***your name*** great" (וַאֲגַדְּלָה שְׁמֶךָ). Not only is this verse (12:2) the third seventh in a series for the word שׁם, but it also marks the *seventh* time the word *bless* appears in the entire Torah! As the Midrash comments on Genesis 2:4, B'HBRAM (בהבראם, when [B] they were created [HBRAM]): "The world was created for the sake of *Abraham*" (אברהם). In Hebrew, ABRHM (אברהם) has the same letters as HBRAM (הבראם). The blessings that God would bestow upon the nations would flow through the children of Abraham.

Symmetry of Blessings

First, Genesis 1:22: God ***blessed*** them, saying, "Be fruitful and multiply, fill the waters in the seas, and let the birds increase on the earth."

1:28: God **blessed** them and God said to them, "Be fruitful and multiply . . . ."

2:3: And God **blessed** the seventh day and declared it holy. . . .

5:2: Male and female He created them, and He **blessed** them. . . .

9:1: God **blessed** Noah and his sons, and said to them, "Be fruitful and multiply, and fill the earth."

9:26: And he said, "**Blessed** be the LORD, The God of Shem . . . ."

Seventh, 12:2: I will make of you a great nation, and I will **bless** you; and I will make your **name** great. . . .

In the first blessing in the Torah, God *blesses* the animals in the sea and sky that they be fruitful and multiply (1:22). At the seventh *blessing* in the Torah, God's *blessing* is that Abram's children would propagate and become a great nation. The generation of the Tower wanted to make *their name* great, but at the seventh שם and the seventh *blessing*, God *blesses* Abram, that *his name* be great and that he would be fruitful and beget a great nation. His blessing is *sevenfold*, having *seven* predicate verbs:

1. And I will make of you a great nation,
2. And I will **bless** you,
3. And I will make your **name** great,
4. And you shall be a blessing.
5. I will bless those who bless you,
6. And he who curses you I will curse;
7. And through you shall all the families of the earth be blessed.   (12:2–3)

Abram אברם
12:1, 4, 4, 5, 6, 7, 9

land ארץ
12:1, 1, 5, 5, 6, 6, 7

bless ברך
12:2, 3, 3, 3; 14:19, 19, 20; 17:16, 16, 20; 18:18; 22:17, 17, 18

In Genesis 12:1–9, the paragraph containing the sevenfold blessing above, both *Abram* and *land* are written *seven* times each. The link between *Abram* to the *Promised Land* is accentuated by the sevenfold symmetry of both words.

In 12:2, the word *bless* appears twice, the first of which marks the *seventh* occurrence of the word *bless* in the Torah, "And I will **bless** you." The second begins another sevenfold unit of blessing, and the *seventh* reflects the *first*:

First: . . . And you shall be a ***blessing***.   (12:2)

Twenty-first in the Torah: And through your seed *shall **all** the nations of the earth be **blessed***, because you hearkened to My voice.   (22:18)

The last of this series is an echo of Abraham's first blessing: "*And through you shall **all** the families of the earth be **blessed**"* (12:2–3).

Symmetry of *All* (כל) in Genesis 5–12

Genesis 5 through 12 recounts the generations of Adam through the arrival of Abraham. Within these chapters, we find another amazing pattern of the word *all* (כל):

First: These are the generations of Adam. When God created man, He made him in the likeness of God; male and female He created them. And when they were created, He *blessed* them and called them Man. When Adam had lived 130 years, he begot a son in his likeness after his image. . . . And ***all*** the days that Adam lived came to 930 years; then he died.   (5:1–5)

The ninety-first *all* (13 × 7th), counting from Genesis 5, is found together with the seventh *blessing*, counting from the beginning of the Torah:

91st (13 × 7th): And ***all*** the families of the earth shall **bless** themselves through you.   (12:3)

The one hundred fortieth *all* (twice 70th), counting from Genesis 5, occurs together with the thrice seventh *blessing*, counting from the beginning of the Torah:

140th (2 × 70th): And ***all*** the nations of the earth shall be ***blessed*** through your seed, because you have hearkened to My voice.   (22:18)

We have before us an amazing overlapping symmetry of *name* (שם), *blessing* (ברך), and *all* (כל). The word שם appears *seven* times in Genesis 10, which tells of the descendants of Noah, *seven* more times in the story of the people of Babel, who wanted to make *their name great,* and six times in the generations of Shem, culminating in a *seventh* at the blessing of Abram, where God says He will make *Abram's name great.* This verse also marks the ninety-first *all* (13 × 7th), counting from the generations of Adam in Genesis 5. In addition, Abram's blessing is the *seventh* time the word *blessing* is used in the Torah:

> I will make of you a great nation, and I will **bless** [7th in the Torah] you; I will make your **name** [21st שם, counting from Genesis 10, the generations of Noah] great, and you shall be a blessing [beginning another sevenfold unit for *bless*]. I will bless those who bless you, and curse him that curses you; and **all** (91st *all,* starting from Genesis 5, the generations of Adam) the families of the earth shall be blessed through you. (12:2–3)

The symmetry continues for *bless* and *all,* when God blesses Abraham after the binding of Isaac.

> And through your seed shall **all** [140th counting from Genesis 5] the nations of the earth be **blessed** [21st in the Torah], because you have hearkened to My voice. (22:18)

The nations of the earth, who are on the level of the *sixth,* the level of the six days of physical Creation, can reach completion only through Abraham, who is on the level of the *seventh,* the level of the Sabbath.

The chart and notes on the next page summarize the symmetrical convergence of these words based upon a pattern of sevens.

	FIRST IN SERIES	BLESSING OF ABRAM Gen. 12:2–3	BLESSING OF ABRAHAM Gen. 22:18
בֵרֶךְ BLESS BLESSED BLESSING	**First *blessing* in Torah:** God created . . . *all* the living creatures with which the waters swarmed, . . . and the birds . . . . And God *blessed** them, saying "Be fruitful and multiply." (Gen. 1:21–22)	**Seventh *bless* in Torah:** I will make of you a great nation, And I will *bless* you; and I will make your *name* great.	**Twenty-first *bless* in Torah:** And through your seed shall *all* the nations of the earth be *blessed,* because you hearkened to My voice.
שֵׁם SHEM NAME THERE	**First שֵׁם in Generations of Noah:** These are the generations of the sons of Noah, *Shem,*** Ham, and Japeth. (Gen. 10:1)	**Twenty-first שֵׁם** from the generations of the sons of Noah, and **seventh,** from the generations of Shem: I will make your *name* (שֵׁם) great.	
כֹּל ALL/EVERY (counting from Gen. 5)	**First כֹּל in Generations of Adam:** And he begot sons and daughters. And *all* the days that Adam lived. (Gen. 5:4–5)	**91st כֹּל (13 × 7th)** And through you shall *all* the families of the earth be **blessed.**	**140th כֹּל (2 × 70)** And through your seed shall *all* the nations of the earth be *blessed,* because you hearkened to My voice.

This first *blessing* comes immediately after the first *all* in the Torah: "God created the great sea monsters, and *all* the living creatures that crawl about, with which the "waters swarmed, after their kind, and *all* winged fowl after their kind, and God saw that it was good, and God *blessed* them . . . ." (Gen. 1:21–22). *All* appears in multiples of seven in Genesis 1, 3, 6, 8, 9, 11, as well as 13 × 7 times in Genesis 5:1–12:3, and 2 × 70 times in Gen. 5–22.

The *seventh* שֵׁם, "These are the sons of *Shem* . . . ." (10:31), echoes the *first,* "These are the generations of the sons of Noah, *Shem* . . . ." (10:1).

The first blessing in the Torah, a blessing of fertility, is bestowed upon the first animals that are created. The same blessing is given to Man: to *be fruitful and to multiply*. *All* the generations of Adam and *all* the generations of Noah's son, *Shem,* culminate in Abram, through whom *all* the generations of Man are to be *blessed*. The Torah teaches these concepts through the numerical symmetry of *Shem, all,* and *blessing,* which unites the creation of *all* the animals, the generations of Adam and *Shem,* and the *blessings* of Abraham.

As already noted, each patriarch receives a sevenfold blessing: Abraham in Genesis 12:2–3, Isaac in 26:3–4, and Jacob, in 27:28–29. That the blessings of Abraham would be passed to Jacob is affirmed when Isaac blesses Jacob with full recognition of the son who stood before him:

> May God Almighty bless you, make you fertile and numerous, so that you become an assembly of peoples. May He grant the blessing of Abraham to you and your offspring, that you may possess the land where you are sojourning, which God assigned to Abraham. (28:3–4)

The purpose of creation, *B'HiBaRAM* (בהבראם), *when they were created* (2:4), would be realized through the generations of Abraham, B'ABRaHM (באברהם).

Chapter 5

Discerning the Tree of Life
through Numerical Symmetry

T HE TORAH IS a Tree of Life, a tree of interconnecting words. In this chapter, we shall review and examine amazing word patterns using a graphic format. By examining these words as they branch out in their numerical patterns, we uncover the beauty and unity of its many branches.

The ensuing graphics illustrate the sevenfold patterns of a sample of words in the Torah, followed by patterns based upon ten and combinations of tens and sevens.

כל *All/Every*

The little word כל (*all/every*) is a fascinating study. It is like a branch of the Tree of Life, climbing its way through the Torah, embracing *all* animals and people, from their creation through their destruction and salvation during the Flood, culminating in the blessing of Abraham, through whom *all* the nations of the earth would be blessed.

On the following pages are two graphics illustrating the use of the word כל "all/every" in the opening chapters of the book of Genesis. Both of these graphics should be read as a tree grows, from the bottom up.

The word כל (*all/every*) begins with a listing of *all* the living creatures in God's creation (Genesis 1:21). At the *seventh*, God provides Man with food from the living bounty of plant life (1:29). Another cycle of seven continues with a listing of all that God created – *all* plants, birds, and *everything* that

כל – All/Every

Genesis 8
All/Every 14X
(8:1,1,9,17,17,17,19,
19,19,19,20,20,21,22)

Fourteenth: While *all* the days of the earth remain, seed time and harvest, cold and heat, summer and winter, and day and night shall not cease. (Gen. 8:22)

Seventh: Every beast, *every* creeping thing, and every bird, and all that creeps upon the earth, after their kinds, went out of the ark. (Gen. 8:19)

First: And God remembered Noah, and *every* living thing. (Gen. 8:1)

Genesis 6
All/Every 14X
(6:2,5,5,12,13,17,17,
19,19,19,20,20,21,22)

Fourteenth: And Noah did according to *all* that God commanded him, so he did. (Gen. 6:22)

Seventh: And, behold, I bring a flood of waters upon the earth, to destroy all flesh, where there is the breath of life, from under heaven; *all* that is in the earth shall die. (Gen. 6:17)

First: The sons of rulers saw the daughters of men that they were fair; so they took as wives from *all* those whom they chose. (Gen. 6:2)

Genesis 3
All/Every 7 X
(3:1,1,14,14,14,17,20)

Seventh: Adam called the name of his wife Eve, for she was the mother of *all* living. (Gen. 3:20)

First: The serpent was more cunning than *all* the beasts of the field which the Lord God had made. (Gen. 3:1)

Genesis 1
All/Every 14X
(1:21,21,25,26,26,28,
29,29,29,30,30,30,30,31)

Fourteenth: And God saw *all* that He had made, and behold, it was very good. (1:31)

Seventh: God said, Behold, I have given you *every* herb bearing seed, which is upon the face of *all* the earth, and *every* tree.... (1:29)

First: God created the great *taninim*, and *every* kind of creature that lives in the waters, and *every* kind of winged bird, and God saw that it was good. (1:21)

א

כל – All/Every (continued)

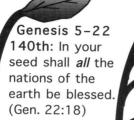

Gen. 20: All 7 X

Gen. 19: All 7 X

Gen. 14: All 7 X

Gen. 9: All 21 X

Genesis 5–22
All/Every 140X

(91 times in Gen. 5 –12:3, plus 49 in Gen. 12:5 –22: Gen. 12:5,20;13:1,9,10, 10,11,15; 14:3,7,11,11, 16,20,23; 15:10; 16:12, 12,12; 17:8,10,12,12, 23,23,23,27; 18:18,25, 26,28; 19:4,12,17,25, 25,28,31; 20:7,8,8,13, 16,16,18; 21:6,12,22; 22:18)

Genesis 5–22
140th: In your seed shall *all* the nations of the earth be blessed. (Gen. 22:18)

Genesis 11
All/Every 7X
(Gen.11:1,4,6,6,8,9,9)

Seventh: Therefore is the name of it called Babel; because the LORD did there confuse the language of all the earth; and from there did the LORD scatter them abroad upon the face of *all* the earth. (Gen. 11:9)

First: And *all* the earth was of one language, and of one speech. (Gen. 11:1)

Genesis 5–12:3
All/Every 91X
(13X7)
Generations of
Adam to Blessing
of Abraham

(Gen. 5:5,8,11,14,17,20,23,27, 31; 6:2,5,5,12,13,17,17,19,19, 19,20,20,21,22; 7:1,2,3,4,5,8, 11,14,14,14,14,14,14,15,16,19, 19,21,21,21,22,22,23; 8:1,1,9, 17,17,17,19,19,19,20,20,21, 22; 9:2,2,2,2,3,3,5,10,10,10,10, 11,12,15,15,15,16,16,17,19,29; 10:21,29; 11:1,4,6,6,8,9,9; 12:3)

Thirteen times seventh: and in you shall *all* families of the earth be blessed. (Gen. 12:3)

First: And *all* the days that Adam lived were nine hundred and thirty years; and he died: And Seth lived a hundred and five years, and fathered Enosh. And Seth lived after he fathered Enosh eight hundred and seven years, and fathered sons and daughters. (Gen. 5:5–7)

א

moves upon the earth. By the *twice seventh* כל, God sees *all* that He had made and declares it to be very good (1:31).

Another cycle of seven occurs in the story of the Garden of Eden. At the *first all/every*, it is stated, "The serpent was more cunning than *all* the beasts of the field." At the *seventh*, Eve is called "the mother of *all* living" – of every human being, whether simple or cunning, good or bad.

In Chapter 6, the corruption of Man begins with the sons of rulers, who "took for themselves women מכל, *from all* of whom they had chosen" (6:2). By the *seventh* כל (*all/every*), it is declared, "*all* that is in the earth shall die" (6:17). But there is hope for mankind and all life when Noah obeys God and does "according to *all* that God had commanded him" (6:22).

> In Chapter 8, "God remembers Noah and *every* living thing" (8:1). At the *seventh* כל, *every* living creature departs from the ark (8:19). By the *fourteenth* כל, God promises to maintain the order of the earth: "While *all* the days of the earth remain, seedtime and harvest, cold and heat, summer and winter, and day and *night* shall not cease" (8:22). (This is the *seventh* time that *night* appears in the Torah. The *first* is in Genesis 1:5, ". . . and to the darkness He called *night*." The rhythm of day and night that marked the beginning of creation is renewed.)

Genesis 9 is the last chapter of *all* the days of Noah, where *all* is written *twenty-one* times. The *thrice seventh all* ends with the death of Noah: "And *all* the days of Noah were 950 years, and he died" (9:29).[32]

The chronology of the generations of Adam begins in 5:1: "This is the book of the descendants of Adam – on the day that God created Man." The word כל appears for the *first* time in this chapter in 5:5:

> *All* the days that Adam lived were nine hundred and thirty years; and he died.

Ninety-one is the product of two significant numbers – *thirteen* and *seven*. The chronology of Man, which begins with "***all** the days that Adam lived*" (5:5), reaches culmination at the *thirteen* times *seventh*, the blessing of Abram:

> And through you shall ***all*** the families of the earth be blessed (12:3).

The symmetry of *all* continues an additional *forty-nine* times through the binding of Isaac, where Abraham receives a renewal of the blessing he had received as Abram.

> Through your seed shall *all* the nations of the earth be blessed...
>
> (22:18)

Continuing the count from the generations of Adam (5:1), we come to the *140th all*:

> And **all** the nations of the earth shall bless themselves through your offspring, because you have listened to My voice.   (22:18)

All that God created, the sevenfold *all* of creation that God sees as very good (1:31), has been created for the sake of Abraham, who will bring fruition to *all the days of Adam's life* (5:5), to the nations that were scattered over the face of *all* the earth (11:9), by bringing *blessings* to **all** *families of the earth* (12:3) and to **all** the nations of the earth (22:18). The sevenfold repetition pattern of the word כל links *all* of creation and *all* of humanity to the blessing that would be vouchsafed *all* the families and nations of the earth through the children of Abraham.

The numerical symmetry of כל, *all/every*, unites the creation of life and the generations of Adam and Noah to the blessings of Abraham. *Everything, when they were created,* בהבראם, *was created for the sake of Abraham,* באברהם, through whom *all the nations of the earth shall be blessed*. The sevenfold symmetry of the little word כל is the Divine thread that binds this all together.

The Brother Narratives in Patterns of Seven

Fraternal relationship is a major theme in the Book of Genesis. This theme is emphasized again and again by a sevenfold repetition of the word *brother*.

The first narrative of sibling rivalry ends in fratricide. Cain kills Abel and Cain flees from the presence of the LORD (4:16). In this episode, the word *brother* appears *seven* times. The *first* and *seventh* are related:

First: And she continued to bear his **brother** Abel. Abel became a shepherd, and Cain became a tiller of the **ground**.   (4:2)

all	כל
	12:5, 20; 13:1, 9, 10, 10, 11, 15; 14:3, 7, 11, 11, 16, 20, 23; 15:10; 16:12, 12, 12; 17:8, 10, 12, 12, 23, 23, 23, 27; 18:18, 25, 26, 28; 19:4, 12, 17, 25, 25, 28, 31; 20:7, 8, 8, 13, 16, 16, 18; 21:6, 12, 22; 22:18

Seventh: "What have you done? The blood of your *brother* cries out to Me from the *ground*. And now you are cursed more than the **ground**, which opened wide its mouth to receive the blood of your **brother** from your hand." (4:10–11)

The *ground* of Cain's labor absorbs his brother's blood and gives testimony to the violence. The blood of his brother transforms the product of his hands. The *ground* of his life's work has become cursed, for all of man's labor is worthless in the face of violence between brothers.

We have seen that the words *man* (אדם) and *ground* (אדמה), which have the same root, appear for a total of *thirty-five* times in the first three chapters of the Torah. In the narrative of Cain and Abel (4:1–24), we find this root an additional *seven* times.

The word *ground* (אדמה) is recorded six times in Chapter 4. The *seventh*, at the birth of Noah, ameliorates the curse of the *ground*:

man   אדם
4:1, 2, 3, 10, 11, 12, 14

ground   אדמה
4:2, 3, 10, 11, 12, 14; 5:29

First: And she continued to bear his *brother* Abel. Abel became a shepherd, and Cain became a tiller of the **ground.** (4:2)

Sixth: And now you are *cursed* more than the **ground**, which opened wide its mouth to receive the blood of your *brother* from your hand. (4:11)

Seventh: And he called his name Noah saying, "This one will bring us rest from our work and from the toil of our hands, from the **ground** which Hashem has *cursed*."[33] (5:29)

The seventh *ground*, relating to Noah, hearkens back to Cain, the first *tiller of the ground*.

The numerical symmetries of the words *brother, ground,* and *man* tie the events of the Garden of Eden, and Cain and Abel, to the birth of Noah.

The three fraternal stories in Genesis all emphasize the word *brother* in multiples of seven. In the story of Cain and Abel, we find *brother seven* times. In the narratives of the birth of Jacob and Esau and their struggle over the blessing, *brother* is inscribed *fourteen* times. When Laban and his kinsmen pursue Jacob, *brother* is written *seven* times. The Jacob and Esau story continues in *Parashat Vayishlach*, where *brother* is written an additional *seven* times. The brother symmetry persists in the Joseph narratives. In Genesis 37, where his brothers sell Joseph, we find *brother twenty-one* times. When the brothers come to Joseph's house in Genesis 44, the word *brother* appears *seven* times. When Joseph reveals himself to his brothers and reunites with his father, in Genesis 45–46, *brother* recurs an additional *fourteen* times. Finally, when Joseph presents his father and brothers to Pharaoh, the word *brother* is written, once more, *seven* times.

In the Torah, words that define major themes are emphasized by the sevenfold appearance of these words. By emphasizing the word *brother* in multiples of seven within all the sections of fraternal conflict, the Torah invites us to connect these stories – to see these stories as a progression. Cain murders his brother Abel. Esau plans to kill Jacob over the blessings. In the end, they embrace, but part company. Joseph's brothers change their plan from murder to selling Joseph as a slave. They reunite in Egypt, embrace, and come together at their father's deathbed, each to receive a blessing. Aaron and his younger brother, Moses, have no conflict. They embrace and remain together.

The phrase, *Aaron your brother*, occurs *seven* times in the Book of Exodus. The first indicates an end to the conflict between an older and younger sibling. Aaron, the older brother, rejoices in the leadership mission of his younger brother.

אהרן אחיך
Aaron your brother
4:14; 7:1, 2; 28:1, 2, 4, 41

First: And He said, "Is there not *Aaron your brother*, the Levite? I know that he will surely speak; moreover, behold, he is going out to meet you, and when he sees you he will rejoice in his heart." (4:14)

The loving relationship between brothers is expressed, again, at the *seventh* time the phrase, *Aaron your brother,* appears in the Book of Exodus.

Seventh: With these you shall dress *Aaron your brother* and his sons with him. You shall anoint them, inaugurate them and sanctify them, and they shall minister to Me. (28:41)

There is no jealousy on the part of Moses, the younger brother, as he dresses and anoints Aaron, the older brother into the priesthood.

Brother

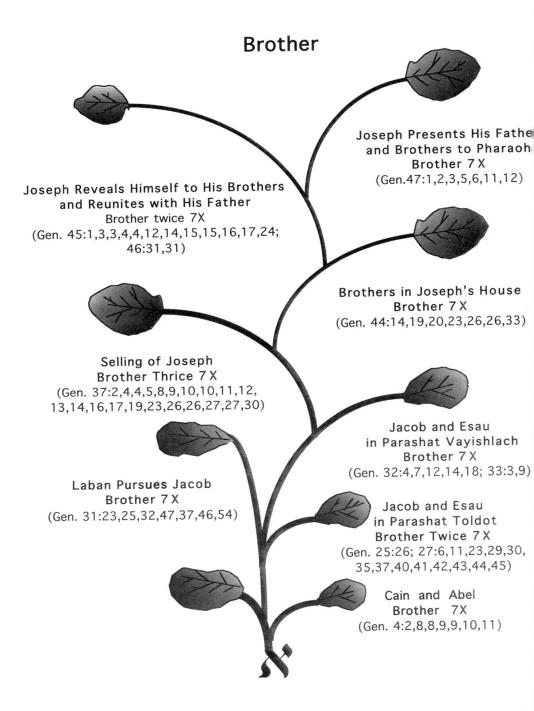

Joseph Presents His Fathe[r]
and Brothers to Pharaoh
Brother 7 X
(Gen.47:1,2,3,5,6,11,12)

Joseph Reveals Himself to His Brothers
and Reunites with His Father
Brother twice 7X
(Gen. 45:1,3,3,4,4,12,14,15,15,16,17,24;
46:31,31)

Brothers in Joseph's House
Brother 7 X
(Gen. 44:14,19,20,23,26,26,33)

Selling of Joseph
Brother Thrice 7 X
(Gen. 37:2,4,4,5,8,9,10,10,11,12,
13,14,16,17,19,23,26,26,27,27,30)

Jacob and Esau
in Parashat Vayishlach
Brother 7 X
(Gen. 32:4,7,12,14,18; 33:3,9)

Laban Pursues Jacob
Brother 7 X
(Gen. 31:23,25,32,47,37,46,54)

Jacob and Esau
in Parashat Toldot
Brother Twice 7 X
(Gen. 25:26; 27:6,11,23,29,30,
35,37,40,41,42,43,44,45)

Cain and Abel
Brother 7X
(Gen. 4:2,8,8,9,9,10,11)

Ten as a Manifestation of Divine Providence

Ten is a significant number in the Torah. The Zohar teaches that there are ten *Sefirot*, ten manifestations of Divine Providence, that affect the worlds. The significance of ten is demonstrated through numerical patterns based upon the number *ten* throughout the Torah.

Tradition teaches that there were *ten* statements of Creation. We find the word ויאמר, *and He said*, *ten* times in Genesis 1. There are *ten* plagues in Egypt and *ten* statements at Sinai. Abraham undergoes *ten* trials. There are *ten* generations from Adam to Noah, *ten* generations from Noah to Abraham, and *ten* generations from Abraham to David.

We find the word דבר, which is often rendered as *speech*, *ten* times in the preparation for the giving of the Decalogue. In the verses that relate the response of the people to the revelation at Sinai, we find דבר *ten* times, again. From the story of the golden calf to the building of the *Mishkan*, דבר is found *thirty* times, three times *ten* (Chapters 31–40). This count lies within a larger section, from the command to build the *Mishkan* to the completion of its construction (Chapters 25–40), where דבר occurs an additional *ten* times, bringing the total to *forty*.[34]

Many of the dimensions of the *Mishkan* are in multiples of *ten*. There are 10 posts, 10 sockets, 50 *gold clasps*, 50 brass clasps, 40 silver sockets, 10 strips of cloth 30 *cubits long*, each with 50 loops, and planks that measure *10* cubits in length. The enclosure of the Tabernacle is 100 cubits on the south side and 100 cubits on the north side, with 20 posts and 20 sockets on each of these sides. The west side is 50 cubits with 10 posts and 10 sockets. The east side is 50 cubits long, too, allowing 20 cubits for the gate. The *tenfold* dimensions of the *Mishkan*, which represents the holiness of the world in microcosm, reflects the macrocosm that was created with *ten* utterances.

As we will note in detail later, in the Torah as a whole, the names of each of the Patriarchs occur in multiples of ten. In addition, the total number of times the four-letter name of the LORD appears in the Torah is a multiple of *ten*, *seven*, and the *twenty-six*, the *gematria* (numerical equivalent) of י־הוה.

Read the Ten graphic on the following page as a tree grows, from the bottom up.

ויאמר
and He said
1:3, 6, 9, 11, 14, 20,
24, 26, 28, 29

speech דבר
Decalogue
prelude
Exodus 19:6, 6, 7,
8, 8, 9, 9, 19; 20:1, 1

speech דבר
Decalogue
aftermath
20:16, 16, 19; 24:3,
3, 3, 4, 7, 8, 14

Ten: Manifestation of Divine Providence

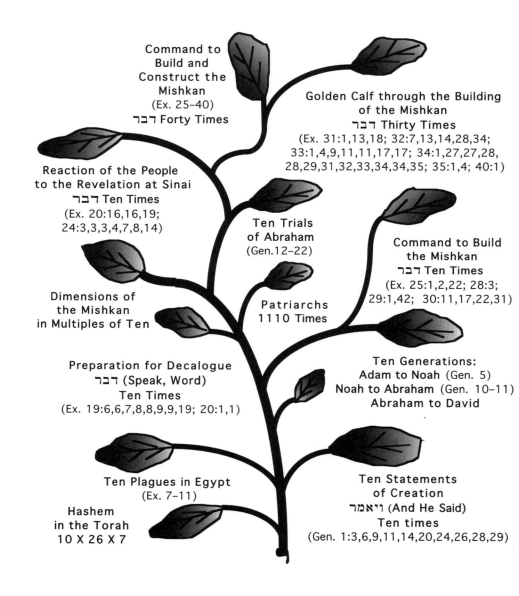

Command to Build and Construct the Mishkan
(Ex. 25–40)
דבר Forty Times

Golden Calf through the Building of the Mishkan
דבר Thirty Times
(Ex. 31:1,13,18; 32:7,13,14,28,34;
33:1,4,9,11,11,17,17; 34:1,27,27,28,
28,29,31,32,33,34,34,35; 35:1,4; 40:1)

Reaction of the People to the Revelation at Sinai
דבר Ten Times
(Ex. 20:16,16,19;
24:3,3,3,4,7,8,14)

Ten Trials of Abraham
(Gen.12–22)

Command to Build the Mishkan
דבר Ten Times
(Ex. 25:1,2,22; 28:3;
29:1,42; 30:11,17,22,31)

Dimensions of the Mishkan in Multiples of Ten

Patriarchs
1110 Times

Preparation for Decalogue
דבר (Speak, Word)
Ten Times
(Ex. 19:6,6,7,8,8,9,9,19; 20:1,1)

Ten Generations:
Adam to Noah (Gen. 5)
Noah to Abraham (Gen. 10–11)
Abraham to David

Ten Plagues in Egypt
(Ex. 7–11)

Hashem
in the Torah
10 X 26 X 7

Ten Statements of Creation
ויאמר (And He Said)
Ten times
(Gen. 1:3,6,9,11,14,20,24,26,28,29)

The Patriarchs

The Patriarchs are the chariot of the *Shekhinah* on earth. The *ten Sefirot* operate through them. Each of the patriarchal names appears in the entire Torah for totals that are multiples of *ten*.

The name of the first patriarch, אברהם/אברם, is inscribed 210 times in the entire Torah, a multiple of both *seven* and *ten* (151 for Abraham, and 59 for Abram).

The word used for Isaac's name, יצחק, which means *will laugh*, appears exactly 100 times, that is, *ten* times *ten*. Ninety-eight times, twice *seven* squared, יצחק refers to Isaac's name, and twice to the meaning of his name – will laugh – in connection with his naming. The context determines whether יצחק is to be read as a name, *Isaac*, or as *will laugh*, but in Hebrew, it is a single word that refers to the Patriarch, and this word/name, יצחק, appears exactly 100 times in the Torah.

Jacob is also called Israel. The exact name Israel, ישראל, appears 587 times in the Torah.[35] Jacob, יעקב/יעקוב is written 213 times. These names total 800 in the entire Torah.

When we add the names of all three Patriarchs together, we get a perfect symmetry based upon the number *ten*. The patriarchal words, אברהם/אברם, יצחק, and יעקב/יעקוב/ישראל total 1110 times in the Torah, that is, $10^3 + 10^2 + 10^1$.

This is an amazing symmetry because it spans the entire Torah, linking the Patriarchs of Israel through a perfect symmetry of tens. *Ten* is the number of *Sefirot*, the number of times God speaks at Creation and at Sinai, and a number that pervades the structure of the *Mishkan*. We find this symmetry throughout the wide expanse of the Torah, providing convincing evidence of the unity of the text.

Total for Patriarchs in the Torah
$$800 + 100 + 210 = 1110 = 10^3 + 10^2 + 10^1$$

יעקב יעקוב ישראל
Jacob/Israel
800 in Torah

יצחק
Isaac/Will–Laugh
100 in Torah
(Words with the letters of
Isaac's name – יצחק –
are inscribed 100 times:
98 times as *Isaac* [2X7^2],
and twice as *will laugh.*
In Hebrew, Isaac's name is
Will–Laugh – יצחק).

אברם אברהם
Abram/Abraham
210 in Torah

It is said that the Patriarchs are the chariot of the *Shekhinah.*
As such, the *tenfold* manifestations of the Patriarchs in the Torah
become a conduit for the *tenfold Sefirot* within this world.

Flow of God's Name through Genesis and Noah

Hashem: 14X in Parashat Noah (Genesis 6:9–11:32)

7X in Noah and the Flood
7X in Nimrod and Babel

Elokim: 7X in Generations of Adam (Genesis 5)

Elokim 7X

Names of God Total 70 in Genesis 1–4

70th: Then began men to call upon the name of Hashem. (4:26)

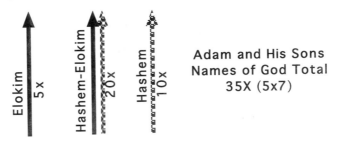

Elokim 5x   Hashem-Elokim 20x   Hashem 10x

Adam and His Sons
Names of God Total
35X (5x7)

35th: ...which Elokim created to do. (2:3)

Elokim 35X

Creation
Elokim 35X (5x7)

1st: In the beginning Elokim created... (1:1)

Hashem in the Book of Exodus

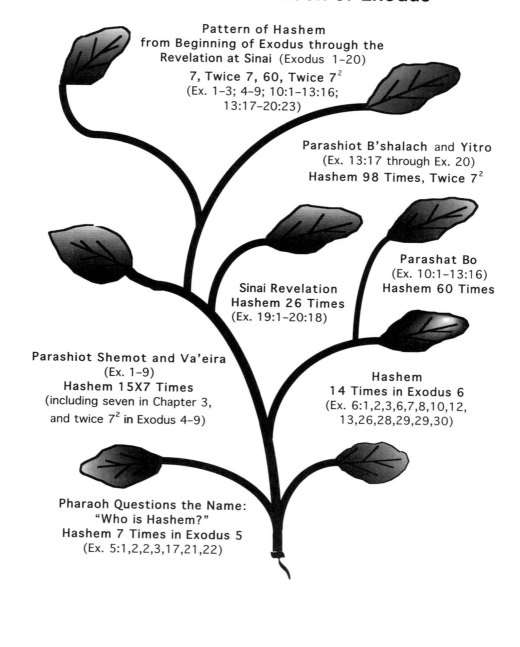

Pattern of Hashem
from Beginning of Exodus through the
Revelation at Sinai (Exodus 1–20)

7, Twice 7, 60, Twice 7^2
(Ex. 1–3; 4–9; 10:1–13:16;
13:17–20:23)

Parashiot B'shalach and Yitro
(Ex. 13:17 through Ex. 20)
Hashem 98 Times, Twice 7^2

Parashat Bo
(Ex. 10:1–13:16)
Hashem 60 Times

Sinai Revelation
Hashem 26 Times
(Ex. 19:1–20:18)

Parashiot Shemot and Va'eira
(Ex. 1–9)
Hashem 15X7 Times
(including seven in Chapter 3,
and twice 7^2 in Exodus 4–9)

Hashem
14 Times in Exodus 6
(Ex. 6:1,2,3,6,7,8,10,12,
13,26,28,29,29,30)

Pharaoh Questions the Name:
"Who is Hashem?"
Hashem 7 Times in Exodus 5
(Ex. 5:1,2,2,3,17,21,22)

Hashem in the Torah
1820 Times

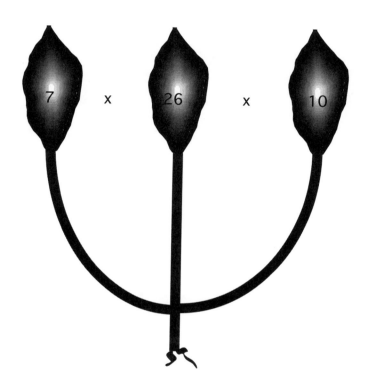

1820
The Four-letter Name of the LORD
1820 Times in the Torah
1820 = 26 X 7 X 10

In the entire Torah, the total for the Tetragrammaton is a product of the *gematria* of the Name – 26, the symbol of holiness – 7, and the number of Divine emanation – 10.

Hashem, the Four-Letter Name of God

In the entire Torah, the four-letter Name of God, (יהוה), appears a total of 1820 times. This count is a multiple of *seven*, but not just any multiple. It is also a multiple of *ten*, the number of Divine utterances at Creation and at Sinai, and the number of *Sefirot* through which Divine Providence is manifest through the worlds, and a multiple of *twenty-six*, the *gematria* (numerical equivalent) of the four-letter Name itself. From the beginning of the Torah to the end, *Hashem* appears in the text exactly $7 \times 10 \times 26$ times, binding the Torah into a perfect unity.

Part Two

Applying Numerical Symmetry to the Study of the Biblical Text

RATHER THAN CONTINUE to catalog sevenfold repetitions throughout the Torah, it would be more useful to examine how we can use numerical symmetry as a tool to analyze the biblical text.

Sensitivity to words is an essential ingredient in the study of biblical passages. Words that reverberate in cycles of sevens are to be understood as a unit. The *first* is connected to the *seventh*. When we come across such a nexus, where one verse is joined to another through numerical symmetry, our perception of the narrative expands.

Parallel texts are supported by numerical symmetry. Numerical symmetries point the way to parallel texts. In the following chapters, we shall observe how simply counting words can expand our grasp of the written Torah.

Chapter 6

A Tikkun: Rebekah and Eve

Introduction

The Torah is an organic whole.* Each section, each word and letter, is interconnected. When we study a particular text in the Torah, we must examine its relationship to the Torah as a whole. A key to finding these relationships lies in listening to the echoes of words and phrases that reverberate from one place to another. The story of Jacob and Esau, and its connection to Eden and Sinai, will serve to illustrate this concept.

The consequences of the events of the Garden of Eden took an historic turn when Isaac blessed Jacob instead of Esau. Isaac had intended to bless Esau, the very son who had just taken wives who "were a bitterness of spirit to Isaac and Rebekah" (Genesis 26:35), but Rebekah knew that the progeny of Esau could not bring the world closer to redemption. Only the nation that would issue from Jacob could become a vessel for Isaac's blessings – both the physical and spiritual heritage of Abraham. Rebekah performed a radical act. She took from the cunning that was the province of the snake of the Garden of Eden, and commanded Jacob to bring savory food to Isaac. In so doing, Rebekah affected a *tikkun* (repair) of the error of her foremother,

---

* This article originally appeared in *Tradition* (27:1, 1992). Some minor changes have been made to fit the theme of this book. In this article, numerical symmetry was not at the center, but the method of counting words was employed to draw connections between verses and themes in the Torah.

Eve. Eve had given her husband, Adam, from the fruit of the tree that the LORD God had commanded not to eat, "*and he did eat* (ויאכל)" (3:6). Rebekah ensured that *her* husband, Isaac, would eat from the savory food of Jacob, a source that was in accord with the will of God, "*and he did eat* (ויאכל)" (27:31). One day, Jacob's progeny would encamp at Sinai and eat from the Tree of Life – the Torah: "and they beheld God, *and they did eat* (ויאכלו)" (Exodus 24:11).

In this chapter, we shall explore the relationship of the story of Jacob and Esau to the narratives of the Garden of Eden and the revelation at Sinai. Our aim is twofold. First, we will demonstrate the remarkable parallels of word, phrase, and numerical symmetry that connect these accounts. Word parallels and numerical symmetries are methods the Torah employs to draw our attention, as if to say, "Do not forget to look at parallel sections when you try to understand the text before you." Second, we will suggest a way to understand the connections between these seemingly unrelated texts. Eve had given Adam from the fruit of the Tree of the Knowledge of Good and Evil, instead of the Tree of Life. Rebekah ensured that *her* husband would eat from the right "tree," from the savory food of Jacob, instead of Esau. As a result, a nation that would be worthy to receive the Torah – the children of Israel, and not the progeny of Esau (or any combination thereof) – would come to Sinai and eat from the Tree of Life. The parallels between the accounts of the revelation at Sinai and the Garden of Eden suggest that at Sinai the human being had returned, at least for the moment, to the spiritual state that had once been his in Eden. Rebekah's *tikkun* had made this possible.

Jacob and Esau, and the Garden of Eden

What basis do we have for connecting Rebekah to Eve, or Isaac's eating of the savory food to Adam's eating of the fruit? When we listen carefully to the story of Jacob and Esau and their struggle for their father's blessing, we can hear the resounding echo of the Garden of Eden. The parallels between the two accounts are quite striking. In the pages that follow, we shall note many of these parallels, as well as explore their implications.

The Generations of Isaac, and the Generations of Heaven and Earth

Let us begin our examination by listening to the opening sentence of each section.

JACOB AND ESAU	THE GARDEN OF EDEN
And these are the generations of Isaac, son of Abraham; Abraham begot Isaac. (Gen. 25:19)	These are the generations of the heavens and the earth when they were created, in the day that the LORD God made earth and heaven. (Gen. 2:4)

The similar assonance of *ve'eleh toldot … ben Avraham* and *eleh toldot … behibaram* is most striking. The Midrash has noted that אברהם (*Abraham*, ABRHM) and הבראם (*they were created*, HBRAM) are anagrams, and we have already noted that in Genesis 2:4 בהבראם, *when they were created*, marks the *seventh* time the word *create* appears in the Torah. The *seventh*, "… when they were *created*, in the day that the LORD God made earth and heaven," is a reverberation of the *first*, "In the beginning God *created* the heaven and the earth." The chronicle of the Garden of Eden is the beginning of the generations of heaven and earth. The history of heaven and earth reaches fulfillment through the generations of Abraham and Isaac. *Parashat Toldot* – the generations of Isaac son of Abraham – deals with the problem of who would inherit the task of bringing the history of heaven and earth to its intended purpose. Would it be Esau, Jacob, or a combination of both?

Also, we should note the similar structure of these opening sentences. Both are made of two clauses, the second of which is a repetition of the first, but in reverse order: "the heaven and the earth when they were created … the LORD God made earth and heaven" and "Isaac, son of Abraham; Abraham begot Isaac."

In addition, it is not fortuitous that the phrase *these are the generations* appears for the *first* time in the Torah at the beginning of the account of the Garden of Eden, and for the *seventh* time at the beginning of the story of Jacob and Esau. *Seven* is a number of completion, and the *seventh* is connected to the *first*. The *tenth* time (corresponding to the *ten* statements of Creation) that the expression *these are the generations* occurs is in *these are the generations of Jacob*, as if to say, *the heavens and the earth that were created for the sake of Abraham reach completion through the generations of Jacob* (2:4; 6:9; 10:1; 11:10, 27; 25:12, 19; 36:1, 9; 37:2).

First: *These are the generations* of the heavens and of the earth when they were created, in the day that the LORD God made earth and the heaven. (2:4)

Seventh: *These are the generations* of Isaac, son of Abraham.... (25:19)

Tenth: *These are the generations* of Jacob.... (37:2)

Esau and the Snake of the Garden

According to the Zohar, Esau is connected to the Snake of the Garden:

"... Esau was drawn after the serpent. ... Jacob knew that Esau was destined to ally himself with that tortuous serpent...."

(Zohar 137b–138a)

There are a number of literary parallels that suggest such a relationship.

The word heel (עקב) is prominent in the account of the birth of Jacob and Esau. This is the second time the Torah employs this word. The first time is in relation to the Snake and the seed of Eve:

JACOB AND ESAU	THE GARDEN OF EDEN
And after that his brother came forth, And his hand was grasping the *heel* of (בעקב) Esau; so he called his name Jacob (יעקב). (Gen. 25:26)	And I will put enmity between you and between the woman, and between your seed and between her seed; it shall bruise your head, and you shall bruise its *heel* (עקב). (Gen. 3:15)

We can better understand the significance of Jacob's grasping the heel of Esau if we look at a third verse. The first time we find the root of the word *grasp* (אחז) is in our verse: "and his hand was *grasping* (אחז) the heel of Esau" (25:26). The second time is when God tells Moses to *grasp* the tail of the snake:

The LORD said to Moses, "Put forth your hand and *grasp* (אחז) it by its tail." (Exodus 4:4)

The heel of a man is analogous to the tail of a snake: Both are at the ends of their respective bodies. If we understand Esau to represent the snake, then the Torah may be suggesting that it is the task of Jacob to grasp the snake by its tail (tail = heel) and, like Moses, to turn the snake into a rod of God: "Moses took the rod of God in his hand" (4:20).

THE TORAH DESCRIBES BOTH ESAU AND THE SNAKE OF
THE GARDEN IN RELATION TO THE FIELD:

THE SNAKE	ESAU
And the Snake was more cunning than all the beasts of the *field* (השדה). (Gen. 3:1)	And Esau was a man who knows[36] trapping, a man of the *field* (שדה). (Gen. 25:27)

The numerical symmetry of the word *field* (שדה) reinforces the connection between these two verses. Counting from "the Snake ... of the *field*" to "Esau, the man of the *field*," we find the word *field* (שדה) *twenty-one* times, that is, three times seven.

field שדה
3:1, 14, 18; 4:8;
14:3, 7, 8, 10; 23:9,
11, 13, 17, 17, 19,
20; 24:63, 65;
25:9, 10, 27

Before Isaac would give his blessing, he told Esau to go to *the field* to hunt for venison:

> And now, if you please, take your gear, your sword, and your bow, and go to *the field* (השדה) and trap for me some game. (27:3)

Isaac sent Esau to *the field* (השדה), the domain where Esau was an expert trapper. According to Rashi, Esau's skill as a trapper was to "trap and deceive his father with his mouth." Esau, the "*man of the field* (איש שדה)", was like the Snake, who "was more deceptive than all the *beasts of the field* (חית השדה)." The *field* was the habitat for both the cunning of the Snake and the guile of Esau.

Isaac had become addicted to the venomous game of Esau: "Now Isaac *loved* (אהב) Esau because trapped game was in his mouth" (25:28). Isaac would eat from this catch, and when his spiritual vision had become sufficiently diminished, he sent Esau to *the field* – to the domain of the Snake. Before Isaac's soul could come to bless Esau, Isaac had to eat, once again, from the trapped game he had come to *love*: "go out to the *field*, and trap for me game; and make me savory food such as I *love* (אהב), and bring it to me that I may eat, that my soul may bless you before I die" (27:3–4). At no other time did a Patriarch ask to eat before he would give a blessing.

That the venom of the Snake had affected Isaac's decision to bless Esau is indicated by the similar language used in Isaac's charge to Esau, and in the Snake's seduction of Eve:

> **Isaac:** And it came to pass, that when Isaac was old and his *eyes* (עיניו) were dimmed from seeing, that he called Esau ... and he said: "Behold, now, I am old, I *know not* (לא ידעתי) the *day* of my *death* (יום מותי). And now ... make me savory food ... that I may *eat* of it (ואכלה), that my soul may bless you before I *die* (אמות)." (27:1–4)

> **The Snake:** And the Snake said to the woman, "You shall surely *not die* (לא־מות תמתון). For God *knows* (ידע) that in the *day* (ביום) that you *eat* (אכלכם) thereof your *eyes* (עיניכם) shall be opened, and you shall be like God *knowing* (ידעי) good and evil." (3:4–5).

Both Isaac and the Snake used the words *know, not, day, eat,* and *die.* The transposed words of the Snake had penetrated the language of Isaac.

The Snake had promised Eve that their eyes would be opened, but when they opened their eyes they knew only that they were naked,[37] and they hid from the presence of the LORD God (3:7–8). Adam and Eve's spiritual vision had, in fact, been dimmed by the cunning of the Snake. Like Adam and Eve, Isaac's spiritual vision had been diminished by the venom of a snake – by the deceptive trappings of Esau as it is written: "and his eyes were dimmed from seeing, and he called Esau" (27:1).

The Association of Eating and Death in Both Stories

Eating is associated with *death* three times in relation to Isaac's eating of the savory food, and three times in relation to Adam and Eve's eating from the Tree of the Knowledge of Good and Evil:

JACOB AND ESAU:

> And make me savory food, such as I love, and bring it to me, that I may *eat* (ואכלה), that my soul may bless you before I *die* (אמות). (27:4)

Bring me some game, and make me savory food, that I may *eat* (ואכלה),
and I will bless you before the LORD before my *death* (מותי).   (27:7)

And I will make of them savory food for your father, such as he loves;
and you shall bring it to your father, that he may *eat* (ואכל) so that he
may bless you before his *death* (מותו).   (27:9–10)

THE GARDEN OF EDEN:

But of the Tree of the Knowledge of Good and Evil you shall not *eat*
(לא תאכל) of it, for in the day that you *eat* (אכלך) thereof *die you shall
die* (מות תמות).   (2:17)

But of the fruit of the tree which is in the center of the garden, God has
said: You shall not *eat* (לא תאכלו) of it, nor shall you touch it, lest you
die (פן־תמתון).   (3:3)

You shall surely not *die* (תמתון לא־מות), for God knows that the day
you *eat* (אכלכם) thereof your eyes shall be opened. . . .   (3:4–5)

Isaac and Rebekah's threefold association of *eating* with *dying* corresponds
to Adam and Eve's threefold association of *eating* with *dying*. Both Adam
and Isaac expected imminent death after eating – Adam, if he would eat
from the Tree of Knowledge, and Isaac, soon after he would eat from the
savory food of Esau. Adam did not die after he had eaten the fruit, but he
lived another 930 years; and Isaac did not die after he had requested savory
food from Esau, but he lived another 57 years. Although Adam did not die
physically on the same day that he ate from the fruit, he did suffer a spiritual
diminution. If Isaac, whose spiritual vision was already weakened, had
eaten, once again, from the catch of Esau, and had transferred his mission,
in whole or in part, to a son who was spiritually connected to the Snake of
the Garden, then Isaac's spiritual blindness would have resulted in spiritual
death, God forbid.

Rebekah had to intervene. She had to ensure that *this* time the man
would eat from a tree of life, instead of a tree of knowledge of good and evil,
from a Jacob, "a wholesome man, dwelling in tents," instead of an Esau, "a
man who knows trapping, a man of the field" (25:27).

Rebekah and Eve

There are a number of parallels that connect Rebekah to Eve. The motif of the Garden of Eden continued to play in the life of Rebekah.

Both Eve and Rebekah are called *mother* (*'em*):

REBEKAH	EVE
Rebekah, *mother of* (אֵם) Jacob and Esau. (Gen. 28:5)	Eve ... *mother of* (אֵם) all living. (Gen. 3:20)

These are the first two times that this precise form of the word *mother*, אֵם, appears in the Torah. Eve, the "mother of all living," is the mother of the macrocosm. Rebekah, as "mother of [both] Jacob and Esau" is mother of the macrocosm, as well. Eve is the mother who conceived her first children in the Garden of Eden, but bore them in exile. Rebekah is the mother whose chosen progeny, the Children of Israel, would show the Children of Adam the way back to the Garden, and to the Tree of Life that stands in its midst.

In order to get Isaac to eat from the savory food of Jacob, Rebekah borrowed from the cunning of the Snake of the Garden, and she disguised Jacob as Esau.

REBEKAH AND JACOB	THE SNAKE
Your brother came with cunning (בְּמִרְמָה),[38] and he has taken your blessing. (Gen. 27:35)	Now the snake was more cunning (עָרוּם) than all the beasts of the field. (Gen. 3:1)

Although מרמה and ערום have different roots, they have similar assonance and a related meaning. The Zohar has already noted the connection between the cunning of Jacob and Rebekah, and the cunning of the snake: "... a woman (pattern of Eve) and a man (pattern of Adam) will circumvent and outmaneuver the evil serpent and him who rides on him" (Zohar 145b).

Rebekah dressed Jacob in garments of skin. The first time in the Torah that we find the roots of the words *skin* (עוֹר) and *clothed* (לבשׁ) is when God clothed Adam and Eve in garments of skin. The second time is when Rebekah clothed Jacob in skins:

REBEKAH AND JACOB	ADAM AND EVE
And Rebekah took the treasured garments of Esau ... which were with her in the house, and she *clothed* (ותלבש) Jacob ... And with the *skins* (ערת), of the kids of the goats she *clothed* (ותלבש) his arms and the smooth of his neck. (Gen. 27:15–16)	And the LORD God made for Adam and his wife garments of *skin* (עור), and He *clothed* them (וילבשם). (Gen. 3:21)

According to the Midrash, Esau's treasured garments, which were kept with Rebekah, were the same garments that God had made for Adam.[39] This Midrash is supported by the fact that the first two times that we find the words *skin* and *clothed* in the Torah are in the stories of Adam and Eve, and Rebekah and her sons. Rebekah dressed Jacob in these vestments from Eden, as if to say, *in the very same skins that Adam wore, when he was expelled from the Garden, shall you wear, when you bring your father the savory food that I have prepared.* The garments that marked man's expulsion from the Garden shall mark the beginning of his return.

The exact same verb forms are used to describe both Eve and Rebekah giving, and Adam and Isaac eating:

REBEKAH AND ISAAC	EVE AND ADAM
And she gave (ותתן) the savory food and the bread, which she had made into the hand of Jacob ... And he brought it near to him [Isaac, Rebekah's husband], *and he did eat* (ויאכל). (Gen. 27:17–25)[40]	*And she gave* (ותתן) also to her husband with her, *and he did eat* (ויאכל). (Gen. 3:6)

Eve and Rebekah *gave*, and Adam and Isaac *did eat*.

However, the ramifications of each eating were not the same. After Adam and Eve had eaten from the forbidden fruit, they suffered a spiritual decline. "The eyes of them both were opened, and they knew that they were naked" (3:8). The spiritual vision that Adam and Eve had once enjoyed was replaced by the physical perception of their own nakedness, and they "hid from the presence of the LORD God." The outcome was very different when Isaac ate the savory food that Rebekah had prepared. Instead of the spiritual fall that Adam and Eve had suffered, Isaac experienced a spiritual rejuvenation. His prophetic vision was restored, and he could smell the Garden of Eden: "*See* (ראה), the smell of my son is as the smell of a field which the LORD has blessed" (27:27). Rashi comments, "there is no smell worse than the smell of washed goatskins! However, this teaches that there entered with him the smell of the Garden of Eden."[41] Isaac's spiritual vision had returned, and he could see the true fragrance of the son who stood before him.

A Tikkun for the Curse of the Ground

The word *give* appears three[42] times in both stories. *Give* appears three times in Chapter 3, beginning with Eve *giving* Adam the fruit: "and she *gave* also to her husband with her, and he did eat" (Genesis 3:6). Eve's *giving* resulted in the cursing of the ground, making difficult the acquisition of grain with which to eat bread: "The woman whom you *gave* to be with me, she *gave* me of the tree, and I did eat" (3:12). "Because you have hearkened to the voice of your wife . . . cursed is the ground for your sake. In toil shall you eat of it all the days of your life . . . and you shall eat the grain of the field. In the sweat of your face shall you eat bread" (3:17–19). *Give* also appears three times in Chapter 27, beginning with Rebekah *giving* Jacob savory food to bring to his father: "And she *gave* the savory food and the bread which she had made into the hand of Jacob, her son" (27:17). Rebekah's *giving* resulted in a blessing of the land, facilitating the acquisition of grain with which to eat bread: "and he blessed him, and said: See, the smell of my son is as the smell of a field which the LORD has blessed. And may God *give* you of the dew of the heavens and of the fat of the earth, and abundant grain and wine. Let peoples serve you [work the land]" (27:27–29). "Behold, a lord I have made him over you, and all his brethren I have *given* to him for servants, and with grain and wine I have sustained him" (27:37).

Eve had *given* Adam forbidden fruit, and a curse was brought into the world. Rebekah *gave* Jacob savory food and bread, so that blessing would be brought into the world. In so doing, Rebekah began to repair the damage inflicted by the sin of her foremother, Eve. As the Zohar states:

> Jacob thus equipped himself with wisdom and cunning, so that the blessings reverted to himself, who was in the image of Adam, and were snatched from the serpent of "the lying lips" [Esau], who acted and spoke deceitfully in order to lead astray the world and bring curses on it. Hence, Jacob came with craft and misled his father with the object of bringing blessing upon the world and recovering from the serpent

what hitherto he had withheld from the world. It was measure for measure . . . From the very days of Adam, Jacob was destined to snatch from the serpent all those blessings, leaving him immersed in curses . . . Jacob turned each curse into a blessing, and he took what was his own. (Zohar 143a–143b)

The Voice of Rebekah and the Voice that Walks in the Garden

In *Parashat Toldot* (Genesis 25:19–28:9), the root of the word *voice* (קוֹל) occurs *seven* times. The first and seventh *voice* is also the first and seventh *hear/hearken* (שמע).[43] The *first* of this double series of seven fixes the essential spirituality of the expression *hearken to my voice* (שמע בקלי):

> Because Abraham *hearkened* (שמע) *to my voice* (בקלי) and kept My charge, My commandments, My statutes, and My Torahs.[44] (26:5)

The first time *hear* and *voice* appear in the Torah is in the Garden of Eden, where these words are found together three times. *Hear* and *voice* are written together three times in the narrative of Rebekah and Jacob, too.[45] Both texts are connected to the concept of mitzvah (commandment).

voice   קוֹל
26:5; 27:8, 13, 22, 22, 38, 43

hear   שמע
26:5; 27:5, 6, 8, 13, 34, 43

REBEKAH AND JACOB	THE GARDEN OF EDEN
And now, my son, *hearken to my voice* (שמע בקלי), to that which I *command* you. Go to the flock and fetch two good kids. (Gen. 27:8–9)	And they *heard* (וישמעו) the *voice* (את־ קוֹל) of the LORD God walking in the garden. (Gen. 3:8)
Upon me be your curse, my son; only *hearken* to my *voice* (שמע בקלי), and go fetch me [them]. (Gen. 27:13)	I *heard* (שמעתי) Your *voice* (קלך), in the garden, and I was afraid. (Gen. 3:10)
And now, my son, *hearken to my voice* (שמע בקלי): arise and flee to Laban, my brother. (Gen. 27:43)	Because you have *hearkened* to the *voice* (שמעת לקול) of your wife and have eaten from the tree which I *commanded* you, saying, "You shall not eat of it," cursed is the ground. (Gen. 3:17)

Rebekah's *voice* is connected to the *Voice* that walks in the Garden, and her *command, hearken to my voice,* is connected to the *command* of God. When

Jacob *hearkened* to his mother's *command* to bring Isaac savory food, he affected a *tikkun*, a repair, of the sin of Adam and Eve.

The Exile of Adam, and the Exile of Jacob

Jacob's exile from the land of Canaan closely parallels Adam's exile from Eden. The same verb, to send (שׁלח), is used to record both exiles.

JACOB'S EXILE FROM CANAAN	ADAM'S EXILE FROM EDEN
And Isaac *sent* forth (וישׁלח) Jacob; and he went to Paddan-Aram .... (Gen. 28:5)	Therefore the LORD God *sent* him forth (וישׁלחהו) from the Garden of Eden .... (Gen. 3:23)

Both exiles are in the *east*:

	JACOB'S EXILE FROM CANAAN	ADAM'S EXILE FROM EDEN
east קדם 2:8, 14; 3:24; 4:16; 10:30; 11:2; 12:8, 8; 13:11, 14; 25:6, 6; 28:14; 29:1	Then Jacob lifted his feet, and he went to the land of the children of the *east* (קדם). (Gen. 29:1)	He drove out the man, and He placed at the *east* (מקדם) of the Garden of Eden the Cherubim. (Gen. 3:24)

Genesis 29:1 is the *fourteenth* time *east* is written in the Torah. The *first* is, "And the LORD God planted a garden in Eden, in the *east*, and placed there the man whom He had formed" (2:8).

Why does the Torah bother to specify the direction of both exiles? The numerical symmetry of *east* directs our attention to an intertextual relationship. Jacob's exile to the children of the east begins a long journey that would one day return the Children of Jacob to the eastern gate of spiritual Eden, when they would come to Sinai and receive the Tree of Life, the Torah. The entrance to the Tabernacle is also in the east. Within the Tabernacle lies the ark with Cherubim atop the ark cover. Within the ark lie the Tablets and the Torah scroll that were given at Sinai, and the Torah is called a *tree of life* (Proverbs 3:18). It is the Cherubim that lie both at the eastern gate of Eden and above the ark cover, and it is "from between the Cherubim" that Hashem imparts words of Torah to Moses (Numbers 7:89). *East* serves as both the exit into exile and the portal of return.[46]

In both texts, we find expressions of *keeping the way, eating bread, return,* and *returning to the ground:*

JACOB'S EXILE FROM CANAAN

And, behold, I am with you, *and I will keep you* (וּשְׁמַרְתִּיךָ) wherever you walk, and *I will return you to this ground* (וַהֲשִׁבֹתִיךָ אֶל־הָאֲדָמָה), until I have done that which I have spoken to you of. (Gen. 28:15)

If God will be with me, *and will keep me in this way* (וּשְׁמָרַנִי בַּדֶּרֶךְ) in which I am walking, and will give me *bread to eat* (לֶחֶם לֶאֱכֹל), and raiment to be clothed in, so that *I return* (וְשַׁבְתִּי) in peace to my father's house [an allusion to the world to come], then shall the LORD be my God. And this stone . . . shall be a house of God . . . . (Gen. 28:20–21)

ADAM'S EXILE FROM EDEN

So He drove out the man; and He placed at the east of the Garden of Eden the Cherubim, and the flaming sword which turned each way to *keep the way* (לִשְׁמֹר אֶת־דֶּרֶךְ) to the tree of life. (Gen. 3:24)

By the sweat of your face *shall you eat bread* (תֹּאכַל לֶחֶם), until you *return to the ground* (שׁוּבְךָ אֶל־הָאֲדָמָה) from which you were taken; for dust you are, [in your life], and to dust [as you are in your life] shall you *return* (תָּשׁוּב) [an allusion to the resurrection of the dead (Malbim)47]. (Gen. 3:19)

Jacob's prayer on his way into exile was an echo from the Garden of Eden. Both narratives share many of the same key words: *keep, way, walking, give, bread, eat, clothe,* and *return.* Jacob asked that God *clothe* him in protective garments, as God had done for Adam and Eve. He asked for *bread to eat,* even if he had to labor in the heat by day and the frost by night (31:39). This was in accord with God's declaration to Adam: "By the sweat of your face shall you *eat bread.*" Jacob asked God to *keep him in the way* in which he was walking, to remain on the path of He who walks in the Garden; and he petitioned God to *return* him in peace to his Father's house, to the place that "shall be a *house of God.*" Before Jacob called, God had already answered:48 "And, behold, I am with you, and I will *keep* you wherever you walk, and I will *return you to this ground,* until I have done that which I have spoken to you of (28:15). God had promised the same to Adam, ". . . until you *return to the ground* from which you were taken" (3:24). Adam was taken away from the ground of the Garden of Eden, and exiled from the Tree of Life. Jacob asked God to *keep him in this way,* and God promised Jacob that he would *return to this ground,* to the place of the Tree of Life, whose way through the *eastern* gate of Eden is kept by the Cherubim. One day, the progeny of Jacob, the Children of Israel, would *eat* from the Tree of Life – the Torah, which is kept by the Cherubim that rest upon the ark cover. The Cherubim, along with the Torah they guard, are found within the midst of the Tabernacle, the *house of God.* Like the Garden of Eden, the Tabernacle's entrance is in the *east* (Exodus 27:13; 38:13–15). Jacob's prayer – to keep him in this way, to return to his Father's house, and to make this place a house of God – was a yearning to return to the spiritual Garden of Eden and to the Tree of Life.

The Garden of Eden, Rebekah, and Sinai

HEARKEN TO MY VOICE

voice   קול
Toldot
26:5, 27:8, 13, 22,
   22, 38, 43

voice   קול
Sinai in Exodus
19:5, 16, 16, 19, 19;
   20:15, 15

voice   קול
**Sinai in Deuter-
onomy**
5:19, 20, 21, 22, 23,
   25, 25

A key to understanding the significance of Rebekah's intervention to ensure Isaac's blessing for Jacob is the word *voice* (קול). When we listen carefully to Rebekah's thrice stated command, "hearken to my voice," we can hear the whisper of the Garden of Eden and the echo of Mount Sinai.

Voice (קול) appears *three* times in the narrative of the Garden of Eden (Genesis 3:8, 10, 17), *seven* times in *Parashat Toldot*, the section that deals with Isaac and Rebekah, and Jacob and Esau, *seven* times in the account of the revelation at Sinai in the Book of Exodus, and *seven* times in the same account in the Book of Deuteronomy. *Three* is a number of emphases, and *seven* is a number of completion and perfection. When the Torah emphasizes the same word in more than one section by threefold, and, especially, sevenfold repetitions, the Torah is calling on us to understand the word's meaning in one place by the light of its context in another.

The context of the first use of a word in the Torah gives us the word's essential meaning. Let us compare how the word *voice* (קול) is used for the *first* time in each of the sections mentioned above:

The Garden of Eden: And they *heard* the *voice* (קול) of the LORD God walking in the garden. [This verse marks the first time that *voice* and *hear* are found in the Torah, and they are found together.]

(Genesis 3:8)

Toldot: And all the nations of the earth shall bless themselves by your seed; because[49] Abraham *hearkened* to My *voice* (בקלי), and kept My charge, My commandments, and My Torahs. (26:4–5)

Revelation at Sinai: And now, if you will indeed *hearken* to My *voice* (בקלי), and you will keep My covenant, then you shall be a precious treasure to Me from among all the peoples. (Exodus 19:5)

Revelation at Sinai: These words the LORD spoke to all your assembly in
the mount out of the midst of the fire, the cloud, and the thick darkness, a great *voice* (קוֹל), and He added no more. And He wrote them
upon the two tablets of stone, and gave them to me.

(Deuteronomy 5:19)[50]

In each of these verses, the first of a threefold or sevenfold unit of the word
voice, the voice is the *Voice* of God. As Adam and Eve had hidden from the
voice of the LORD after they had eaten from the forbidden fruit, "And they
heard the *voice* of the LORD God walking in the garden ... and the man
and his wife hid themselves from the presence of the LORD God" (Genesis
3:8), so did the LORD's *voice* become hidden from Isaac when he decided
to bless Esau. God's name was not mentioned when Isaac told Esau, "Make
me savory food ... that I may eat, that my soul may bless you before I die"
(27:4). Rebekah, however, never lost her sense of God's presence. When she
overheard Isaac speaking to Esau, she knew that this was not an accident. She
knew that God had wanted her to hear this conversation for some purpose.
Therefore, she took action, adding the LORD's name when she told Jacob, "I
heard your father speaking[51] to your brother Esau, saying, 'Bring me venison, and make me savory food, that I may eat and bless you before the LORD
before my death.' And now, my son, hearken to my *voice* (שמע בקלי) according
to that which I command you. Go now to the flock ..." (27:6–9). Rebekah's
awareness of the Divine presence in the world was rooted in her being.

Three times did Rebekah tell Jacob, *hearken* to my *voice* (27:8, 13, 43);
three times did the Torah record *hear* and *voice* together in the account of
the Garden of Eden (3:8, 10, 17); and *three* times do we find *hear* and *voice*
together in *Parashat Yitro*, the *parashah* of the revelation at Sinai (Exodus
18:19, 24; 19:5).[52] When Rebekah said to Jacob *hearken to my voice*, at once
her soul adhered to the *Voice* that walks in the garden (Genesis 3:8), as well
as to the *Voice* that emanates from Sinai (Exodus 19:5). Rebekah ensured
that Jacob, her son who was so connected to the aspect of *voice*, as in "the
voice is the *voice* of Jacob" (Genesis 27:22), would be the sole recipient of
the heritage of Abraham and Isaac. As Jacob heeded the *voice* of his mother,
so, too, would Jacob's progeny hearken to a *voice* – to the *Voice* of Hashem
at Sinai.[53]

(Rebekah's command to hearken to her *voice* never called for deception, only to go to the flock and bring Isaac savory food. The *voice* of Rebekah never commanded Jacob to wear a disguise. It was Jacob's own anxiety that first suggested the need for deception: "Perhaps my father will feel me . . . ." [27:12]. It was only after Jacob had already hearkened to his mother's voice and had brought the goats, that Rebekah dressed Jacob as Esau [27:14–16]. The spiritual *voice* of Rebekah stated the desired end – that Jacob should bring savory food to his father, and that Isaac should bless Jacob, instead of Esau, but this Divine *voice* within Rebekah never demanded that deception be used to reach this end.)

See the "Voice of God" graphic on the following page. Read the graphic as a tree grows, from the bottom up.

Rebekah, Sinai, and the Return to the Tree of Life

The revelation at Sinai returned the Children of Israel to the spiritual state that had once existed in the Garden of Eden. Many of the words that describe this experience (in Exodus 24:3–18) – *voice, hear, saw, sent forth His hand, eat, dwelt, give, eyes, six days, seven days,* and *in the midst of* – resonate with the echo of Eden. These key words from the account of the revelation at Sinai are essential to the narration of Days Six and Seven, and the Garden of Eden: *voice* (Genesis 3:8, 10, 17), *hear* (3:8, 10, 17), *saw* (1:25, 31; 3:6), *send forth his hand* (3:22), *eat* (1:29, 30; 2:9, 16, 16, 17, 17; 3:1, 2, 3, 5, 6, 6, 6, 11, 11, 12, 13, 14, 17, 17, 17, 18, 19, 22), *dwell* (3:24), *give* (1:29; 3:6, 12, 12), *sixth day* (1:31), *seventh day* (2:1, 2, 3), *eyes* (3:6), and *in the midst of* (2:9; 3:3, 8).

The events in the Garden of Eden took place on the *sixth day* of Creation, and Adam and Eve were sent out before the onset of the *seventh day;* the cloud covered Mount Sinai *six days,* and the LORD called out to Moses to enter on the *seventh day* (Exodus 24:16). God had "caused to *dwell* (וישכן) at the east of the Garden of Eden the Cherubim . . . to guard the way to the Tree of Life" (Genesis 3:24); but "the glory of the LORD *dwelt* (וישכן) upon Mount Sinai . . . and He called to Moses" [to receive the Torah, which is called a Tree of Life] (Exodus 24:16). "The Tree of Life [was] *in the midst of the Garden* (בתוך הגן)" (Genesis 2:9); and Moses entered "*into the midst of the cloud* (בתוך הענן)" (Exodus 24:18). At the gates of Eden, God had placed the "flaming sword that turned each way" (Genesis 3:24); but, at Sinai, it

The Voice (קוֹל) of God

Revelation at Sinai in Deuteronomy
Voice 7 X
(Deut. 5:19,20,21, 22,23,25,25)

First: These words the Lord spoke to all your assembly in the mount out of the midst of the fire, the cloud, and the thick darkness, with a great voice, which was not heard again; and He wrote them on two tablets of stone, and delivered them to me. (Deut. 5:19)

Revelation at Sinai in Exodus
Voice 7 X
(Ex. 19:5,16,16,19,19; 20:15,15)

First: Now therefore, if you will hearken to My voice, and keep My covenant, then you shall be My own treasure among all peoples; for all the earth is Mine. (Ex. 19:5)

Parashat Toldot
Voice 7 X
(Gen. 26:5; 27:8,13,22,22,38,43)

First: Because Abraham hearkened to My voice, and kept My charge, My commandments, My statutes, and My Torahs. (Gen. 26:5)

The Garden of Eden
Voice 3 X
(Gen. 3:8,10,17)

First: And they heard the voice of the Lord God moving in the garden... (Gen. 3:8) was the glory of the LORD that appeared "as a devouring fire" (Exodus 24:17). In the Garden, Eve *saw* that the Tree of the Knowledge of Good and Evil was a "delight to the *eyes* (עין)" (Genesis 3:6); but, at Sinai, it was the glory of the LORD that was *seen* "by the *eyes* (עין) of the Children of Israel" (Exodus 24:17). In the Garden, Adam had *hearkened* (שמע) to the voice of his wife (Genesis 3:17); but at Sinai, the Children of Israel pledged to *hearken* (שמע) to the word of God (Exodus 24:7). In Eden, the LORD had said, "lest he *send forth his hand* (פן־ישלח ידו), and take also from the Tree of Life, and *eat* (ואכל), and live forever" (Genesis 3:22); but, at Sinai, "He did not *send forth His hand* (לא שלח ידו)"[54] and allowed the nobles of Israel to "behold God, and they did *eat* (אכל)" (Exodus 24:11). Adam and Eve had eaten from forbidden fruit, as it is written, "Have you *eaten* (אכלת) from the Tree which I commanded you not to *eat*?" (Genesis 3:11); but the children of Israel *ate* from the peace-offerings of the covenant at Sinai,[55] as it is written, "and they sacrificed peace-offerings of oxen to Hashem. . . . And Moses took the blood, and he sprinkled it upon the people, and he said: 'Behold the blood of the covenant, which the LORD has made with you' . . . and they beheld God, and they did *eat* (ויאכלו) and drink" (Exodus 24:5–11). The descendants of Jacob had been given a taste of the Tree of Life, as the Zohar states:

> When Israel stood before Mount Sinai, the impurity of the serpent was removed from them . . . and in consequence they were able to attach themselves to the Tree of Life.[56]   (Zohar 1:52b)

The descendants of Jacob "*saw* the God of Israel" (Exodus 24:10). They did not hide from the face of God, like Adam and Eve, nor were they spiritually sightless like Isaac (when he decided to bless Esau). They did not eat from that which was forbidden, but from that which was permitted. They were not given from the Tree of the Knowledge of Good and Evil, but were given "tables of stone and the Torah" (24:12). They were not driven from the Garden of Eden, but one man of Israel, Moses, was beckoned to enter the Garden – "Come up to me into the mount" – and take the Torah, the Tree of Life, to the children of Israel, that he might "teach them" (24:12). And Moses entered "into the midst of the cloud (בתוך הענן)" (24:18) to receive the source of life that is "in the midst of the Garden (בתוך הגן)" (Genesis 2:9).

None of this could have happened had Rebekah not acted, had Jacob not *hearkened* to his mother's inner *voice*, her *kol*. Rebekah said, שמע בקלי, *hearken to my voice,* to my inner being that is connected to the *Voice* that walks in the Garden, and to the *Voice* that reveals itself at Sinai.[57] Rebekah employed a similar style of language to command Jacob to *hearken* to her *voice* as Moses used to command the children of Israel to *hearken* to the *Voice* of Hashem. Rebekah said:

> And now, my son, *hearken to my voice to that which I command you*
> (שמע בקלי לאשר אני מצוה אתך).　　　　　　　　　(Genesis 27:8)

Moses said:

> If you will indeed *hearken to the voice* (אם־שמוע תשמע בקול) of Hashem
> your God, to keep and to do all His commandments *which I command*
> *you* (אשר אנכי מצוך) this day.　　　　　　　(Deuteronomy 28:1)

Because of Rebekah's courage to act, Isaac *did eat* (ויאכל) and *did drink* (וישת)[58] from Jacob, the son whose essence was of the aspect of *voice*. One day, Jacob's progeny, the Children of Israel, would *eat* and would *drink* from the Tree of Life, the Torah, for it is written that at Sinai "they beheld God, and they did *eat* (ויאכלו), and they did *drink* (וישתו)," and in the very next verse it is written, "Come up to me into the mount . . . and I will give you the tables of stone, and the Torah, and the *commandments* which I have written" (Exodus 24:11–12).

The revelation at Sinai is connected to the Garden of Eden, and the *voice* of Rebekah is connected to both.

* * *

We have noted numerous parallels between the stories of Jacob and Esau, the Garden of Eden, and the revelation at Sinai. The connections between these texts are too numerous and powerful to be fortuitous. The Torah wants us to understand the story of Rebekah and her sons in relation to Eden and Sinai. We have suggested one way to understand this relationship.

Rebekah's daring intervention was a critical turning point in the movement of the history of heaven and earth, which began in the Garden of Eden, toward the event that would be essential to the fulfillment of that history, the giving of the Torah at Sinai. Eve had given Adam fruit from the wrong tree, from the Tree of the Knowledge of Good and Evil, instead of the Tree of Life. Isaac intended to eat savory food from the wrong son, from Esau, instead of Jacob. This time the woman would give the man food from the right "tree." Rebekah ensured that *her* husband, Isaac, would eat savory food from their righteous son, and would bless Jacob, instead of Esau. In so doing, Rebekah performed a *tikkun* of the sin of her foremother, Eve.[59] If not for Rebekah, Esau would have shared with Jacob the heritage of Abraham and Isaac,[60] and the nation that would bring Torah into the world would never have existed, God forbid. Only the progeny of Jacob, the nation of Israel, could receive the Torah and "eat and drink" (Exodus 24:11) from this Tree of Life. Through the keeping of Torah, the Children of Israel would ensure that one day the Children of Adam would be redeemed from their exile and would "return to the ground from which they were taken" (Genesis 3:19), to the spiritual *ground* of the Garden of Eden. Rebekah's radical act had cosmic consequences. It prepared the way for the ultimate redemption of man and the fulfillment of Creation.

Chapter 7

Numerical Convergence in Genesis 32:22

A REMARKABLE INSTANCE OF numerical symmetry converging in one verse is Genesis 32:22:*

וַתַּעֲבֹר הַמִּנְחָה עַל־פָּנָיו וְהוּא לָן בַּלַּיְלָה־הַהוּא בַּמַּחֲנֶה

And the offering passed over before his face, while he lodged that night in the camp.

(32:22)

At first glance, this verse seems rather unexciting. Jacob is returning from his exile in Paddan-Aram to the land of Canaan, bringing with him his family, servants, and livestock. He encounters a group of angels, and he says, "This is a *camp* (מַחֲנֶה) of God," and he names the place *twin camps* (מחנים) (32:3). Jacob sends messengers [lit. angels] *before him* (לפניו) to his brother, Esau (32:4), and the messengers report that Esau is heading towards him with four hundred men (32:7). Jacob is exceedingly afraid, so he divides the people with him and his livestock into two *camps* (32:8) (מחנות), and he says, "If Esau comes to one *camp* (מחנה) and smites it, then the *camp* (מחנה) which remains will survive" (32:9). Jacob prays to the God of his fathers, "... with my staff I passed over this Jordan; and now I have become two *camps* (מחנות). Deliver me, I pray, from the hand of my brother, from the hand of

---

* Much of the content of this chapter, as well as Chapter 2, has been adapted from the author's series of articles, *Numerical Symmetry: A Method for Learning the Biblical Text*, in *Nishma Journal*, Vols. 2–5, 1988–1989.

Esau: for I fear him, lest he will come and *smite* me, mother with children . . ." (32:11–12).[61] Jacob *lodges* (ילן) *there that night* (32:14) (בלילה ההוא), and he prepares an *offering/gift/tribute* (מנחה) of five hundred fifty animals to be sent ahead to Esau (32:14–17) in the hope that Esau would forgive him for taking the blessing of their father: "I will appease *his face* with the *offering* that goes ahead of *my face*; afterward, when I see *his face*, perhaps he will *lift my face* (32:21). Then comes our verse, *And the offering passed over before his face, while he lodged that night in the camp* (32:22).

On a simple level, this verse serves as a transition, bridging the preparations that Jacob makes before meeting his brother to both the spiritual wrestling he would have later that night and the actual encounter he would have with Esau the next morning. However, the remarkable numerical symmetry of the verse suggests that there is a lot more going on here than merely a link between two phases in the Jacob and Esau saga. Counting from the beginning of the Torah, almost every word appears here for the *seventh* time (or a multiple of seven)! By connecting the *first* appearance of each of these words to its *seventh*, we uncover an extraordinary relationship between our verse and other sections of the Torah.

A Process of Discovery

I first studied Genesis 32:22 while preparing for a Bible class given by Rabbi Murray Schaum at the Hebrew Institute of Riverdale. I noticed that this verse had two key words from the chapter we had been studying, and that both words, *offering* (מנחה) and *camp* (מחנה), are composed of the same letters. Recalling that *camp* (מחנה), occurs at the beginning of the chapter, where Jacob encounters a *camp* of angels, I decided to count the number of times *camp* is written in the chapter. The total came to *seven*, with the seventh in our verse. These were the first times the word *camp* appears in the Torah. Intrigued, I decided to count the word *offering* (מנחה) as well. I found *offering* only four times in the chapter. Was there a seven count for *offering* over a larger expanse of text? I decided to do something I had never done before – count a word from the beginning of the Torah. The count of the word *offering* (מנחה) came to *seven*, four times in our chapter, and three times in the story of Cain and Abel.

At this point, I decided to count the other words in our verse, starting

camp   מחנה
32:3, 3, 8, 9, 9, 11, 22

offering   מנחה
4:3, 4, 5; 32:14, 19, 21, 22

from the beginning of the Torah. What I found was astonishing. Each word I counted had a numerical symmetry based on *seven*.

Night (לילה) appears in our verse for the *twenty-first* time in the Torah. Genesis 32:22 marks the *seventh* time the word *night* is written in conjunction with the word הוא or ההוא (*that night*). In addition, this verse marks the *seventh* time *night* occurs in narratives of Jacob in exile. Our sages teach us that Jacob was a man of the *night*, the founder of evening prayer.

Pass over (עבר), as a verb, makes its *fourteenth* appearance in the Torah in our verse. It marks the *seventh* time *pass over* appears in conjunction with Jacob, and the third time in Genesis 32 (three for emphasis).[62]

The word *his face* (פניו), with those exact letters,[63] is written for the *seventh* time in the Torah in Genesis 32:22. Our verse marks the third time *his face* (פניו) appears in the chapter, and the third time the phrase *on his face* (על-פניו) occurs in the Torah (17:3, 17; 32:22).[64] Verses 32:14–22 (the second *aliyah* in *Parashat Vayishlach*) form a literary unit, beginning with, "And *he lodged there that night*," and ending with "and *he lodged that night* in the camp." In this unit, different forms of the word *face* occur *seven* times, culminating again in our verse (32:17, 18, 21, 21, 21, 21, 22).[65]

Lodged (לן) is the only key word in Genesis 32:22 that does not appear there for a seventh time, when counting from the beginning of the Torah. Our verse marks its ninth appearance. However, *lodged* does occur *seven* times (the *seventh* in our verse) in narratives that deal with the patriarchal family's relationship with Laban – three times when Abraham's servant goes to Laban to get a bride for Isaac (24:23, 25, 54), and four times during Jacob's journeys to and from Laban (28:11; 31:54; 32:14, 22).

Torah and the Law of Entropy

With the exception of *lodged*, as discussed above, all the major words in Genesis 32:22 appear in this verse for a seventh time in the Torah, or a multiple of seven. When we count from the beginning of the Torah to this verse, we find *offering seven* times, *camp seven* times, *his face* (פניו) *seven* times, *pass over fourteen* times, and *night twenty-one* times. The two words whose counts are multiples of seven – *night* and *pass over* – are used in our verse for exactly the *seventh* time in the Torah in conjunction with Jacob.

---

night לילה
1:5, 14, 16, 18; 7:4,
12; 8:22; 14:15;
19:5, 33, 34, 35;
20:3; 26:24; 30:15,
16; 31:24, 39, 40;
32:14, 22

(ב)לילה ההוא/הוא
that night
14:15; 19:33, 35;
26:24; 30:16;
32:14, 22

pass over עבר
8:1; 12:6; 15:17;
18:3, 5, 5; 23:16;
30:22; 31:21, 52,
52; 32:11, 17, 22

his face פניו
4:5; 17:3, 17; 31:21;
32:21, 21, 22

lodged לן
19:2, 2; 24:23, 25,
54; 28:11; 31:54;
32:14, 22

In addition, this verse marks the *seventh* time in the Torah that *night* (לילה) appears together with הוא or ההוא, and the *seventh* time in the paragraph that we find the root of the word *face* (פניו).

Is all this an accident, some statistical coincidence? One might argue that although the odds against any word appearing for the seventh time (or multiple thereof) are seven to one, and that the odds for five such words appearing in the same verse increase geometrically (7^5, or 16,807 to 1). (Actually, the odds are much greater, when you take into account the other sevens mentioned above).[66] Such an eventuality is statistically possible at some point in all the many verses of the Torah. However, when we look at the juncture in the Torah wherein this "coincidence" occurs, five words reaching their state of completion at their *seventh* appearance in a verse that is a state of completion in its own right, when we examine the location of their *first* appearance in the Torah, the *firstness* which conceives the life-force of each word, and when we probe the remainder of this section, Jacob's wrestling with the angel and his final encounter with Esau, and find every one of these words appearing there for an "eighth" time, the *eighth* (seventh plus *one*) symbolizing a spiritual leap beyond time and space, we become awed by all these inconceivable interrelationships and by the meticulous care with which each word of the Torah is written.

The law of probability resists this numerical symmetry. So does the law of entropy. Entropy is the tendency in nature for reduced differentiation, for total randomness and disorder, for *tohu* and *bohu* (Genesis 1:2). A drop of ink placed in a tank of water does not remain a distinct drop of ink, but mixes completely and randomly with the water in the tank. Creation is a process of increased differentiation. Each step in the seven days of Creation moves the world away from *tohu* and *bohu*, from a state of random chaos, towards a more ordered state. The Sixth Day culminates in Man, the most differentiated of God's creatures. The Seventh Day extends the movement towards greater differentiation to the level of *kedushah*, to sanctity. The human being, by observing the Sabbath, by observing the finely differentiated laws of the Torah, can act as co-creator with God and move the world to a higher level of differentiation, to the *kedushah* of the Seventh Day. There is a tradition that God looked into the Torah and created the world. The differentiation within our ordered world reflects the ultimate differentiation within the Torah itself, within the world of *halakhah* (Torah law). The laws of probability and entropy would act to oppose the numerical symmetry that is exemplified by our verse, but the Torah, as the blueprint of Creation, acts to advance this ordered cycle of sevens.[67]

* * *

By attending to the numerical arrangement of the Torah's words, we not only reveal the exquisite Artistry inherent in the Text, but we begin to uncover the intricate interrelationship between various sections of the Torah. Each word of the Torah has a life force of its own. Each word's *first* appearance in the Torah and the context thereof gives us the word's essential meaning, and, perhaps, its mission. The *seventh* indicates a state of completion, as in the completion of creation on the Seventh Day. The *eighth* is beyond the natural world, when each word, having reached its completion in this world, manifests its essence within a purely spiritual plane, or within the context of the Messianic Age. Simply by counting words, by noting the relationship of the *first* occurrence to the *seventh*, we can come to a more expansive comprehension of the biblical text.

Let us examine each of the words in Genesis 32:22, in the essence of its *first* appearance, the completion of its *seventh*, and the spiritual leap of its *eighth*.

* * *

Applying the Method of Numerical Symmetry to the Analysis of a Specific Verse, Genesis 32:22

וַתַּעֲבֹר הַמִּנְחָה עַל־פָּנָיו וְהוּא לָן בַּלַּיְלָה־הַהוּא בַּמַּחֲנֶה

And the offering passed over before his face, while he lodged that night in the camp. (Genesis 32:22)

In the sections that follow, we will use the method of numerical symmetry to locate texts that are parallel to the verse we are studying. In so doing, we will not only come to a fuller understanding of each word in this verse, but we will come to see the significance of this verse in relation to the Book of Genesis as a whole.

Offering (מנחה) and His Face (פניו)

To begin, we shall examine the words *offering* (מנחה) and *his face* (פניו). Not only do both these words appear together for the *seventh* time, counting from the beginning of the Torah, but these words are found together in their *first* appearance in the Torah, as well:

Seventh: And the *offering* (מנחה) passed over before *his face* (פניו).

(32:22)

First: And it was after a period of time, that Cain brought of the fruit of the ground an *offering* (מנחה) to the LORD.[68] And Abel, he also brought of the firstlings of his flock and of the fat thereof. And the LORD turned to Abel and to *his offering* (מנחתו); but to Cain and to *his offer-ing* (מנחתו) He did not turn. And Cain became very angry, *and his face fell* (ויפל פניו).   (4:3–5)

This concurrence of two words, *offering* and *his face*, in both their first and seventh occurrences in the Torah, demands a complete examination of the context within which these words live. The numerical symmetries in the Torah serve as guideposts, pointing the way to verses and sections that need to be compared. When we examine the contexts of the first and seventh appearances of *offering* and *his face*, we find remarkable literary parallels. In both cases, an older brother is jealous of a younger brother. Cain kills Abel. Esau wants to kill Jacob. If we look at the texts carefully, we find *every verse* in the Cain and Abel narrative to have a parallel of similarity or contrast in the Jacob and Esau saga.

BIRTH OF CAIN AND ABEL	BIRTH OF JACOB AND ESAU
Now the man had known Eve, *his wife* (אשתו), *and she conceived* (ותהר) *and she bore* (ותלד) Cain; *and she said* (ותאמר): "I have acquired a man *with the* LORD (את-יהוה)."[69] And she increased *to bear* (ללדת) *his brother* (אחיו) Abel. (4:1–2)	And *she conceived* (ותהר), Rebekah *his wife* (אשתו). And the children struggled within her; *and she said* (ותאמר), "If so, why am I thus?" And she went to inquire *of the* LORD (את-יהוה). . . . And when her days *to bear* (ללדת) grew full, then behold, twins were in her womb. And the first came out red . . . and they called his name Esau. And after that came out *his brother* (אחיו), and his hand grasped Esau's *heel* (בעקב); and his name was called *Jacob* (יעקב). (25:21–26)

The births of Cain and Abel, and Jacob and Esau use many identical words: *his wife, conceived, to bear, his brother, and she said,* and the unusual phrase, *with/of Hashem* (את־י־הוה). The parallels of these opening passages suggest a relationship between these two pairs of brothers. Also, Jacob's grasping of the *heel* of Esau (בעקב) hearkens back to the Snake in the Garden: "You shall bruise its *heel* (עקב)" (3:15).

* * *

There is a parallel construction reporting the occupation of the brothers: *and Abel was . . . but Cain was; Esau was . . . but Jacob was.* Both pairs of brothers are presented with contrasting vocations: shepherd – farmer, hunter – tent-dweller.

And Abel was (ויהי־הבל) a keeper of sheep, *but Cain* (וקין) was a tiller of the ground. (4:2)	*. . . and Esau was* (ויהי עשׂו) a man who knows hunting, a man of the field; *but Jacob* (ויעקב) was a wholesome man, dwelling in tents.[70] (25:27)

* * *

The episodes of the first offering to God and the savory food to Isaac begin with the expression ויהי, *and it was*, after a period of time.

And it was (ויהי) at the end of many days. . . . (4:3)	And it was (ויהי) that when Isaac was old. . . . (27:1)

* * *

Cain *brought* an offering to the Lord, and Abel, *he also brought*:	**Jacob *brought* savory food and wine to his father, and Esau, *he also made and brought*:**
And Cain brought (ויבא) . . . to the Lord. And Abel, he brought also (הביא גם־הוא). (4:3–4)	And he [Jacob] came (ויבא) to his father . . . and he brought (ויבא) to him . . . And he [Esau] made also (גם־הוא), and he brought (ויבא) to his father. (27:18, 25, 31)

The parallel phrases suggest a connection between Cain and Abel's bringing of an offering to their Father in heaven, and Jacob and Esau bringing savory food to their father on earth.

* * *

There is a qualitative difference in the offerings of Cain and Abel:	There is a qualitative difference in the verbal tone of Jacob and Esau, when they bring food to their father:
Cain brought *from* the fruit of the ground. (4:3)	And Jacob said to his father: "... I have done as you have told me. Arise, *please*, *sit*, and eat of my venison ...." (27:19)
And Abel, he also brought of the *firstborn* of his flocks and from their *choicest*. (4:4)	And he [Esau] said to his father, "Arise my father and eat from the venison of his son ...." (27:31)

Abel brings from the best of his flock, Cain from whatever was at hand. Jacob speaks gently to his father – "Arise, please, sit, and eat." Esau's tone is more abrupt: "Arise ... and eat." Jacob goes to the flock and takes two *good* kids of the goats, שני גדיי עזים טבים (27:9), from which his mother cooks the meat that his father *loves*, כאשר אהב. The word *good* that is associated with Jacob's venison is lacking in Esau's.

* * *

The LORD accepts Abel's offering, but not Cain's:	Isaac eats from Jacob's venison, but not Esau's:
The LORD had regard for Abel and his offering, but to Cain and his offering He had no regard. (4:5)	[Jacob] brought it close to him and he ate ... and he blessed him. (27:25) And he said [to Esau regarding Jacob], "Indeed he shall be blessed." (27:33)

After eating the savory food, Jacob approaches Isaac, and kisses him. Isaac's spiritual eyes are opened, and he blesses Jacob saying, "*See*, the smell of my son is like the smell of a field that the LORD has blessed. So may God give you ...." Isaac blesses Jacob, and when Esau arrives with venison from his hunt, Isaac does not eat of it. Instead, Isaac confirms the blessing given to Jacob saying, *Indeed he shall be blessed*, גם־ברוך יהיה. In each sibling story, one brother's efforts are accepted, and the other rejected.

* * *

Both Cain and Esau react with great emotion upon being upstaged by their younger brother.

Cain was very angry.... (4:6)	Esau ... cried with a great and bitter cry. (27:34)

* * *

The acceptance of Abel's offering and the rejection of Cain's cause Cain's face to fall:

And Cain was very angry, and his *face fell,* (ויפלו פניו). And the LORD said to Cain: "Why are you angry, and why is your *face fallen* (נפלו פניך)?" (4:5–6)

In order to have his own face lifted, Jacob sends Esau an offering that is intended to appease Esau's face:

... I will appease *his face* (פניו) with the *offering* that goes before *my face* (לפני), and afterwards I will see *his face* (פניו), perhaps he will *lift my face* (ישא פני). And the *offering* passed over *before his face* (על־פניו). (32:21–22)

Taken together, the pair of parallel segments above emphasizes *face seven* times, with a contrast between *falling* of *face* and *lifting* of *face*.

* * *

Surely, if you will do well (תיטיב), you will be uplifted (שאת). But if you do not do well (תיטיב).... (4:7)

For I fear him, lest he come and strike me ... And you said, "I will surely do you good (היטב איטיב)...." (32:12–13)

In both texts, God promises to do *good* to the individual. However, the promise to Cain is conditional. *Uplift* to Cain depends upon doing good and keeping away from sin. Similarly, Jacob fears that God's promise to him is conditional. He is apprehensive that he might have sinned, thereby forfeiting God's protection.[71] The double use of *good* in both texts emphasizes the *uplift* that comes from doing good. Cain is very angry and *his face falls* (4:6) (ויפלו פניו). God tells Cain, "If you do *good* you will be *uplifted* (שאת)." Jacob sends an *offering* to Esau hoping to appease him: "perhaps he will *lift my face* (אולי ישא פני)" (32:21).

* * *

Desire and kiss have a similar assonance, sharing two letters in their root (שק).[72] God tells Cain that he can rule over the desire to sin. At the height of the deception, Jacob kisses his father – the first kiss in the Torah.

Sin couches at the door; and to you is its *desire* (תשוקתו), but you may rule over it" (4:7)

And *kiss* me (ושקה־לי), my son. And he came near and *kissed* him (וישק־לו)[73] (27:26–27)

At the seventh *kiss* in the Torah, all in the story of Jacob and Esau, Jacob "bows low to the ground *seven* times," and Esau *kisses* Jacob. The first *kiss,*

kiss   שק
27:26, 27; 29:11, 13; 31:28; 32:1; 33:4

the *kiss* of deceptions, is transformed at the seventh, into a *kiss* of reconciliation.

* * *

Both the offerings of Cain and Abel and the venison that Jacob and Esau bring to Isaac lead either to fratricide or the threat of fratricide, with word parallels between both episodes.

And Cain *said* (ויאמר) to Abel *his brother* (אחיו); and it was when they were in the field, that Cain rose up against Abel, *his brother* (אחיו), *and slew him* (...ויהרגהו).   (4:8)

Where (אי) is Abel your brother? (4:9)

And He said: "What have you done (עשית)?"   (4:10)

And Esau *said* (ויאמר) in his heart: "Let the days of mourning for my father draw near, *and I will slay* (ואהרגה) Jacob, my brother (אחי)."   (27:41)

Who—where (מי־אפוא) is he....?   (27:33)

And Jacob said to his father: "I have done (עשיתי) as you have told me."   (27:19)

Every verse in the Cain and Abel narrative continues to have parallels to the account of Jacob and Esau.

* * *

Jacob's *voice* is connected to the *voice* of Abel, and Esau's *hands* are linked to the *hands* of Cain.

The *voice* (קול) of your brother's blood cries out (צעקים) to Me from the ground ... which has opened her mouth to take your brother's blood from *your hand* (מידך).   (4:10–11)

The voice is the voice of Jacob (הקל קול יעקב), *but the hands are the hands of Esau* (והידים ידי עשו).   (27:22)

The spiritual *voice of Jacob* is connected to the voice of Abel, whose offering is pleasing to God. At one point, the spiritual *voice* within Esau cried out, too (27:34) (ויצעק צעקה), saying, "Have you but one blessing, my father? Bless me, even me also, my father. And Esau lifted up his *voice* (קלו), and wept" (27:38). Immediately, Divine blessing flowed down upon Esau in the form of Isaac's blessing (27:39–40). However, Esau's flirtation with the spiritual was short-lived. The spiritual voice within Esau was muted by his suffocating hatred for Jacob: "But Esau hated Jacob because of the blessing wherewith his father blessed him. And Esau said in his heart [instead of raising his voice to God, he addressed the darkness within his heart], "Let the days of mourning for my father draw near; then I will slay Jacob, my brother" (27:41).

* * *

The ground *takes* the *blood* of Abel from the *hand* of Cain. Jacob and Esau reconcile as Esau *takes* the *offering* from the *hand* of Jacob. The *offering* that Jacob gives to Esau becomes a *tikkun* for the *offering* that induces Cain to kill Abel. The *taking* of *blood* from the *hand* of Cain is transposed into the *taking* of *blessing* from the *hand* of Jacob.

And now cursed are you from the ground, which has opened her mouth *to take* (לקחת) your brother's blood *from your hand* (מידך). (4:11)[74]	And Jacob said [to Esau], "... *then take* (ולקחת) my offering from my hand (מידי) ... Please *take* (קח) my blessing that is brought to you ...." And he urged him, and he *took* (ויקח). (33:10–11)

* * *

Beginning with the *hands* that spill Abel's blood, we come to the *seventh hand,* which reflects the *first:*

hand   יד
4:11; 5:29; 8:9;
9:2, 5, 5, 5

First: Cursed are you from the ground, which has opened its mouth to *take* your brother's *blood* from your *hand* (מידך). (4:11)

Seventh: Your *blood* of your lives I will require a reckoning ... and at the *hand* (ומיד) of every man's brother will I require the life of man. (9:5)

The word *hand* appears *seven* times in *Parashat Toldot:*

hand   יד
25:26; 27:16, 17,
22, 22, 23, 23

First: and *his hand* (וידו) was grasping the heel of Esau. (25:26)

Seventh: for *his hands* were like the *hands* of (ידיו כידי) Esau, his brother. (27:23)

The *hand* that had grasped the heel of his brother, in an attempt to be born first, becomes disguised as the *hands* of Esau, in an effort to receive the blessing of the firstborn.

    The next appearance of *hand* begins another unit of *seven* wherein the *seventh* is an echo of the *first.*

hand   יד
30:35; 31:29, 39;
32:12, 12, 14, 17

First: *And he* [Jacob] *gave* [the flocks] *into the hand of* his sons (ויתן ביד בניו).

(30:35)

Seventh: *And he gave* [the herds] *into the hand of* his servants (ויתן ביד עבדיו) (32:17), (who are to tell Esau that the animals are an *"offering* sent to my lord Esau"* [32:19]).

The flocks that Jacob places in the *hands* of his sons are the manifestation of the physical blessing that he had received from his father. Jacob sends, through *the hands of his servants*, a significant portion of this blessing to his brother (an *offering* sent to my lord Esau).

The next appearance of *hand* in the Torah, on the level of the *eighth*, appears together with the *eighth* appearance of *offering* in the Torah:

The eighth: Pray, if I have found favor in your eyes, then *take* my *offering* from my *hand* (ולקחת מנחתי מידי). (33:10)

The first *offering* leads to fratricide and the *curse* of the ground, which had *taken* the blood spilled by the *hand* of Cain. The eighth *offering*, the manifestation of Jacob's *blessing*, is *taken* by Esau from the *hand* of Jacob, leading to reconciliation between brothers.

* * *

For Cain, the land is cursed:

And now, *cursed* are you from the ground, which has opened her mouth ... When you work the ground, it shall no longer yield its strength to you. (4:11–12)

For Jacob, the land is blessed:

See, the smell of my son is as the smell of a field that the LORD has *blessed*. May God give you of the dew of heaven, and of the fat of the earth, and plenty of grain and wine. (27:27–28)

* * *

Cain is sent to wander the earth:

A fugitive and a wanderer shall you be in the *earth* (בארץ). (4:12)

Esau is promised a dwelling on earth:

Behold, of the fat places of the *earth* (הארץ) shall be your dwelling. (27:39)

* * *

Cain says that his sins are too great to bear:

My sin is *greater* (גדול) than I can bear. (4:13)

Jacob fears that his merits have been diminished through sin:[75]

I have been made smaller (קטנתי) by all the kindnesses and the truth you have done with your servant. (32:11)

* * *

Cain fears being slain for murdering his brother. Esau contemplates murdering his bother.

And it will come to pass that whoever finds me will *slay me* (יהרגני). (4:14)

Behold, your brother Esau is comforting himself regarding you *to slay you* (להרגך). (27:42)

* * *

Cain is protected from retribution by the threat of a *sevenfold* penalty. By bowing *seven* times, Jacob assuages Esau's fratricidal anger.

Therefore, whoever slays Cain, vengeance shall be taken on him *sevenfold* (שבעתים). (4:15)

And he bowed to the ground *seven times* (שבע פעמים), until he came near to his brother. (33:3)

* * *

Cain is exiled for murdering his brother. Jacob flees because he has angered his brother, who designs to kill him. Both *go out* to *lands* in the *East*.

And Cain *went out* (ויצא) from the presence of the LORD. (4:16)

And Jacob *went out* (ויצא) from Beersheba, and went toward Haran. (28:10)

And he dwelt in the *land* of (בארץ) Nod, *east* of Eden (קדמת־עדן). (4:16)

Jacob lifted his feet and went to the *land* of the children of the *east* (ארצה בני־קדם). (29:1)

* * *

God decrees a curse upon Cain. Cain pleads with God to moderate the decree. God moderates the decree, and allows Cain to *dwell* in the land of Nod:

[THE DECREE] "And now cursed are you from the ground, which

Isaac decrees that the blessing that Jacob took would remain intact. Esau pleads for a moderation of the decree. Isaac moderates the decree, and blesses Esau with a *dwelling*:

[THE DECREE] "Indeed, he [Jacob] shall be blessed."

opened its mouth to receive your brother's blood from your hand. When you work the ground, it shall no longer yield its strength to you. A fugitive and a wanderer shall you be in the earth."

[THE PLEA] And Cain said to the LORD: "My sin is greater than I can bear. Behold, you have banished me from the face of the land, and from Your face I shall be hid; and I shall be a fugitive and a wanderer on the earth; and it shall be that whoever finds me will slay me."

[MODERATION OF THE DECREE] The LORD said to him, "Therefore, if anyone kills Cain, sevenfold vengeance shall be taken on him." And the LORD put a mark on Cain, lest anyone who met him should kill him. Cain left the presence of the LORD and *dwelt* in the land of Nod, east of Eden.   (4:11–16)

[THE PLEA] When Esau heard the words of his father, he cried with a great and bitter cry, and said to his father: "Bless me, me also, my father."

[DECREE RESTATED] "Your brother came with guile, and has taken your blessing."

[PLEA RESTATED] "Haven't you reserved a blessing for me?"

[DECREE ELABORATED] "Behold, I have made him your lord, and all his brothers have I given to him for servants ... What then can I do for you, my son?"

[FINAL PLEA] "Have you but one blessing, my father? Bless me, me also, my father . . . ."

[MODERATION OF THE DECREE] "Behold, your *abode* shall be the fat of the earth ... but you shall serve your brother. And it shall be when you shall break loose, that you shall shake his yoke from off your neck."   (27:33–40)

* * *

Offering (מנחה) appears for the first three times in the Torah in the Cain and Abel narrative. (4:3, 4, 5)

Offering (מנחה) does not appear again until the Jacob and Esau narrative, where it occurs for the *seventh* and *eighth* times in the Torah. (32:14, 19, 21, 22; 33:10)

The only other time the word *offering* (מנחה) is written in Genesis is in the story of Joseph and his brothers, where it occurs four more times (43:11, 15, 25, 26), making the total in the Book of Genesis *twelve*, a sexagesimal number corresponding to the *twelve* sons of Jacob. In Genesis 43, the chapter that tells of the *offering* that the brothers bring to Joseph, we find many words and phrases that resound from the Jacob and Esau narrative: *bowed down, your servant, lifted his eyes, made haste, his brother, wept, lodging, firstborn, in their hand, his face, came near, by himself,* and *offering.* The saga of brother stories in the Book of Genesis is bound by the use of similar words and phrases in each.

* * *

The numerical symmetry of the word *brother* emphasizes the relationship between Jacob and Esau, and Cain and Abel.

Brother is written *seven* times in the Cain and Abel story.

Brother, as it relates specifically to Jacob and Esau, occurs *fourteen* times in *Parashat Toldot* and *seven* times when they meet again in *Vayishlach*.

As we have noted earlier, we find the same pattern in the Joseph saga, where *brother* appears in multiples of seven in the many chapters that tell of the selling of Joseph and his encounters with his brothers in Egypt (Chapters 37, 44, 45, 46, 47).

brother אח
(Cain and Abel)
4:2, 8, 8, 9, 9, 10, 11

brother אח
(Toldot)
25:26; 27:6, 21, 23, 29, 30, 35, 37, 40, 41, 42, 43, 44, 45

brother אח
(Vayishlach)
32:4, 7, 12, 14, 18; 33:3, 9

* * *

Our sensitivity to the numerical symmetry of two words – *offering* (מנחה) and *his face* (פניו) – occurring together in both their *first* and *seventh* appearances in the Torah, has led to an examination of the context of each. What we found is extraordinary. The Cain and Abel, and Jacob and Esau narratives are linked by similarities and contrasts in word, theme, and style, as well as in the sevenfold repetition of *brother* in both sections. Every verse in the Cain and Abel narrative has a parallel in the Jacob and Esau saga. Although the odds are against two words – in this case five words – occurring together for the seventh time in the Torah in a single verse, and the odds are magnified against the same two words making their first appearance together, as well, the literary interconnections between the sections containing this *first* and *seventh* suggest that there is no element of chance operating here – only methodical intention.

Without doubt, the *offering* of Cain and Abel is connected to the *offering* that Jacob sent to Esau, but in what way? The *first* appearance of a word in the Torah establishes the word's essential meaning. The context of the first occurrence of *offering* is an offering to the LORD (4:3). At its sublimest level, according to the Malbim, an offering to God is a statement "that God is the cause underlying all causes and their final purpose and justification, and that therefore everything that happens should be associated with Him alone.

... The essential aim of a sacrifice is to express man's submission to God, to benefit his own soul by thinking of the offering as a sacrifice of himself to God."[76] The phrase *offering to the LORD* suggests this sublime mission – the bringing of oneself closer to God, but the first offering's imperfections brought fraternal jealousy and fratricide, instead. For Cain, this first offering caused a *falling* of *his face* (4:5). The *seventh* offering, the offering of Jacob, comes to repair the imperfections of the *first*, and to heal, through the *lifting* of *face*, the falling out between the two brothers.

In order to understand the nature of this repair, we must understand the relationship between the words *offering* (מנחה) and *his face* (פניו), both of which are found together in their first and seventh appearances in the Torah. The first *offering* – Cain's – was incomplete, and caused a *falling of his face*:

> But to Cain and to his *offering* He did not turn. And Cain became very angry, *and his face fell* (ויפלו פניו).
>
> (4:5)

face פנה
1:2, 2, 20, 29; 2:6;
3:8; 4:5

This verse marks the *seventh* time the root of the word *face* (פנה) appears in Genesis. *Offering* and *his face* reach a state of completion at the point of their *seventh* appearance in the Torah, when Jacob finishes his preparations and sends Esau *the offering for the sake of his face* (המנחה על־פניו):

> And he lodged there that night (וילן שם בלילה ההוא), and took from what had come into his hand an *offering* (מנחה) for Esau his brother. ... And he delivered [the animals] into the hand of his servants ... and he said to his servants: *Pass over before my face* (עברו לפני). ... And he commanded the first saying: "When Esau, my brother, meets you, and asks you saying: 'Whose are you, where are you going, and whose are these that are before *your face* (לפניך),' then you shall say: 'They are your servant, Jacob's. It is an *offering* sent to my lord, to Esau, and, behold, he also is behind us'. ... In this manner shall you speak to Esau when you find him. And you shall say, 'Moreover, behold, your servant Jacob is behind us.' For he reasoned, "I will appease *his face* (פניו) *with the offering* that goes *before my face* (לפני, for the sake of *my face*), and afterwards I will see *his face* (פניו); perhaps he will *lift my face* (ישא פני)." So *the offering* (המנחה) passed over *for the sake of his face* (על־פניו), while he lodged that night in the camp.
>
> (32:14–22)

In the paragraph above, which begins and ends with parallel sentences that are centered on the word *offering*, we find the root of the word *face* (פנה) *seven times*! This symmetry suggests that the Torah wants us to understand *offering* and *face* together. The first *offering*, which led to the falling of *his face* (פניו) and to fratricide, has been transformed into the seventh *offering*, which appeases *his face* (פניו) and brings brotherly reconciliation.

The seventh *offering*, then, is a repair of the first. To fully comprehend the essence of this repair, we need to understand the blemish of the first. It is well known that Cain's offering was lacking, that he offered inferior fruit (Rashi), but there was something amiss in Abel's as well. As an offering, Abel's was perfect. Nonetheless, there was in Abel's relationship to his elder brother, perhaps, a lack of humility, a sense of pride in having upstaged Cain. There is no direct textual evidence for this assertion, only that Cain spoke to Abel (4:8) – conversation unrecorded. We can imagine what Cain might have said to Abel – expressions of anger toward his younger brother. Either Abel did not reply, or the Torah did not deem Abel's reply worthy of mention. In any case, Abel lacked the sensitivity to understand his brother's hurt feelings, and to say or do anything that would assuage his anger. Cain did not kill Abel in the heat of the moment (immediately after the offerings), as it is written, "And Cain spoke to Abel his brother; and it came to pass when they were in the field that Cain rose up against Abel his brother and slew him" (4:8). Abel had time to do something constructive to heal his relationship with his brother, to avert his own death and Cain's status as exiled murderer, and to save his parents from the calamity which Rebekah would fear: *Why should I be bereaved of both of you in one day?* (27:45). It was with Cain's own free will that he rose up against his brother Abel, and slew him. However, it may be that God's protective providence would not have been withdrawn from Abel had Abel not committed some sin.[77] Abel had no sin in his relationship between man and God, as it is written, "and the LORD turned to Abel and to his *offering*" (4:4). Abel must have come up short in his relationship between man and man, perhaps in the areas of humility and sensitivity to his brother's feelings, as suggested above.

It is these very areas that Jacob has to address, as well. Like Abel, Jacob is not lacking in his man/God relationship. Like Abel, he needs to soothe the hurt feelings of his brother, to perfect his man/man relationship. Jacob acquires this growth in human relations, combining the inner-directed spiritual strength of his father, Isaac, with the outer-directed loving kindness of his grandfather, Abraham, through Jacob's experience with Laban in exile, and through his preparations to confront his brother, Esau. Jacob completes this growth at the point where *the offering passed over before his face, while he lodged that night in the camp* (32:22). The *offering* to God, which was perfected by Abel, has become perfected on the human level, as well. At its *seventh* appearance in the Torah, *offering* has reached completion.

Simply by noting the first and seventh appearances of two words – *offering* and *his face* – we have come to better understand the significance of Jacob sending המנחה על־פניו, *the offering before his face* (32:22). Jacob was doing more than just assuaging Esau's anger with a *gift* (as *minchah* is often translated). Jacob's *tribute* to Esau was connected to the *offerings* of Cain and Abel. The first *offerings* had led to a falling of face, *and his face fell* (ויפלו פניו) (4:5). The seventh *offering*, the *offering* of Jacob to Esau, would lead to a *lifting* of face: *I will appease his face with the offering* (אכפרה פניו במנחה) *that goes before my face, and afterwards I will see his face – perhaps he will lift my face* (אולי ישא פני) (32:21). The *seventh offering* is a repair of the *first*. Through the symmetry of these words, the Torah is teaching us that our service in this world, our *minchah*, must be directed to both our Father in heaven and our brother on earth.

The Level of the Eighth

Up to this point, we have analyzed the symmetry of words in the Torah based on the number *seven*. *Seven* is a number of completion, as in the completion of Creation in *seven* days. The *first* sets the pattern that is completed at the *seventh*. There is a level that is above the *seventh*, a level that is beyond the physical world, and that is the level of the *eighth*.

The Eighth Offering

After Jacob sends his offering to Esau – *and the offering passed over before him, while he lodged that night in the camp* – *offering* is ready to reach the level of the *eighth*, to that which is above the natural order.[78] At its *eighth* appearance in the Torah (7th + 1), we find *offering* associated with *face* one more time – this time with both the *face* of Jacob's brother, and the *face* of God.

> And Jacob said [to Esau]: No, please, if now I have found favor in your eyes, then take *my offering* (מנחתי) *from my hand*, inasmuch as I have seen *your face* (פניך), which is like seeing the *face of* (פני) God, and you were appeased by me. Please take *my blessing* (ברכתי) that is brought to you, because God has been gracious to me, and because I have everything. And he urged him, and he took. (Genesis 33:10–11)

Offering reaches the level of the *eighth*, the level of the Divine, when Jacob is able to see the spark of God in the *face* of his brother, and to share the physical *blessing* that Jacob had taken from him.

Esau receives Jacob's offering during the night – during the same night that Jacob wrestles with Esau's guardian angel (Rashi).[79] Jacob struggles with this angel until the breaking of the dawn (32:25). At the end of this encounter, it is written:

> And Jacob called the name of the place *Peniel* (פניאל), *Face of God*, for I have seen God *face to face* (פנים אל־פנים), and my life is preserved. (32:31)

The *eighth offering* – "take my *offering* from my hand, inasmuch as I have seen your face, which is like seeing the face of God" – is connected to Jacob's encounter with the Divine, to the angel that he sees "face to face." When Jacob says "take my offering from my *hand*," he is taking the level of *hands*, as in the "*hands* are the *hands* of Esau," and as in "cursed are you from the ground which has opened her mouth to take your brother's blood from your *hand*," and he is raising this level of *hands* to the level of the Divine, to the level of *Voice*, as in "the *voice* is the *voice* of Jacob." Similarly, *offering* undergoes such a transformation, from the *offering* that leads to jealousy and fratricide at its *first* appearance, to the *offering* that brings brotherly reconciliation at its *seventh*. The concept of *offering* reaches the level of the *eighth* when Jacob realizes that his obligation to maintain the highest level of ethical behavior with his fellow man is one with his obligation to serve God:

> Please, no, if I have found favor in your eyes, then take my *offering* from my hand, inasmuch as I have seen *your face*, which is like seeing the *face of God*, and you were pleased with me. (33:10)

This culminating verse, where Jacob sees his brother as an image of God, has 3 × 7 words and 77 letters.

The Essence of Face (פנה)

As we have seen, *offering* is closely connected to *face*. The first appearance of *his face* (פניו), in that exact form, occurs together with the first three appearances of *offering* (4:3–5). *Offering* and *his face* make their seventh appearance in the Torah in the same verse (32:22). The *eighth* time we find *his face* in the Torah (together with the last four occurrences of *offering* in the Book of Genesis) is in the section dealing with the reconciliation of Joseph with his brothers, the final fraternal saga in the Book of Genesis:

> And he [Joseph] washed *his face* (פניו), and came out; and he restrained himself. . . . (43:31)[80]

A few verses prior, we find the brothers approaching Joseph with an *offering* in a manner that is reminiscent of Jacob coming to Esau:

> And when Joseph came home, they brought him *the offering* (המנחה) which was *in their hand* (בידם) into the house, *and they bowed down* (וישתחוו) to him *to the earth* (ארצה). (43:26)

> . . . and he [Jacob] *bowed down* (וישתחו) *to the earth* (ארצה) seven times, until he came near his brother. . . . And Jacob said: ". . . take my offering (מנחתי) from my hand (מידי), forasmuch as I have seen your face. . . . (33:3–10)

Within this chapter of the Joseph story (Genesis 43), there are many other words and phrases that reverberate from the Jacob and Esau saga (*face, ate, drank, brother, Israel, die, offering, man, rise, God, father, asses, bowed down to the ground, cried,* and *his face*). We will not attempt to analyze the parallels between the story of Joseph and his brothers and the other stories of sibling rivalry, except to note one point. Jacob, the potential victim of fratricide, brings an *offering* to appease the potential killer: "Then I will *slay* (ואהרגה)

Jacob" (27:41). Joseph's brothers, the potential killers – "and let us slay (ונהרגהו) him" (37:20) – bring an offering (מנחה) to Joseph to appease the potential victim of fratricide. The simple counting of words strengthens the bond between these narratives of sibling strife.

* * *

In all the other tabulations in Genesis 32:22, we counted the roots of words. Therefore, in addition to looking at the exact word *his face* (פניו), it is proper to examine the appearances of the *root* of the word *face* (פנה), as well. If we count the appearances of the *root* of the word *face*, from the *beginning* of the Torah, we find that our verse, 32:22, "*And the offering passed over before his face* (על־פניו) marks the ninetieth *face* (a sexagesimal number).[81] The *ninety-first* appearance of the root of the word face in the Torah, that is, the thirteen times seventh,[82] is the name *Peniel* (פניאל), literally, *Face of God*:

> And Jacob called the name of the place *Peniel* (פניאל). . . .   (32:31)

The next occurrence of *face*, on the level of the *eighth* (13 × 7th + 1, or 12 × 7th + 8), is the expression *face to face* in the continuation of the verse:

> . . . for I have seen God *face to face* (פנים אל־פנים). . . .   (32:31)

If we exclude *Peniel* from the count, because it is a proper noun having two roots, then *face to face* is both the 13 × 7th and 13 × 7th + 1. Of the two *faces* in the expression, the first is the face of spiritual man. The second face is the encounter with the Divine. This is in keeping with the position that the *eighth* reaches a spiritual plane that is beyond the physical world. The only other times the phrase *face to face* occurs in the Torah are in Exodus 33:11, "And the LORD spoke to Moses *face to face*, as a man speaks to his friend," and in Deuteronomy 34:10, "And there arose not a prophet in Israel like Moses, whom the LORD knew *face to face*."

In order to understand the inner meaning of *face*, we need to examine its *first* appearance in the Torah:

> Now the earth was unformed and void, and darkness was upon the *face* of (על־פני) the deep; and the spirit of God hovered over the *face* of (על־פני) the waters.[83]   (Genesis 1:2)

The *deep* and the *waters* refer to the first elemental forms of matter, the material of the physical world. The darkness, which covers the face of the created world, refers to the concealment of God. God makes room, so to speak, to allow for Creation, and this is the meaning of the *darkness* – the concealment of God's light. But God's presence, though hidden, is near, hovering over Creation: "And the spirit of God hovered over the *face* of the waters." *Face*, then, is the *interface* between the physical world and the spiritual. It is the point wherein the Divine spirit and the human spirit "touch," so to speak. Through the proper service of God, as well as love of one's brother – both of which are symbolized by *offering* (מנחה) – man's face can be lifted:

> Why is your *face fallen*? If you do well, you will be *uplifted* (שׂאת) (4:6–7).

And when man does well, the LORD's blessing flows down through the medium of *face*:

> May the LORD bless you, and keep you. May the LORD make *His face* (פניו) light upon you, and be gracious unto you. May the LORD *lift up* (ישׂא) *His face* (פניו) unto you, and grant you peace.
>
> (Numbers 6:24–26)[84]

This level of *face* is reached after Jacob's *offering* passes over for the *sake of his face* (על-פניו), for the sake of the *lifting* of the *faces* of both Jacob and Esau – *perhaps he will lift my face* (Genesis 32:21) – and after Jacob succeeds in his wrestling with the angel at night. At the *thirteen times seventh* appearance of the root of the word *face* in the Torah, Jacob calls the name[85] of the place *Peniel* (*Face of God*). Jacob merits a face-to-face encounter with the Divine because he has striven with both angels and men, and he has prevailed (32:29). The encounter between the human and the Divine, between the created and the Creator, reaches the level of the *eighth* in:

> ... for I have seen God *face to face* (פנים אל-פנים). (32:31).

The verse immediately following states:

> And the sun rose upon him as he passed over[86] *Peniel* (פנואל) (*Face of God*). (32:32)

The darkness, which conceals the "face of God hovering over the waters," is penetrated by light:

> And Jacob lifted *up* his eyes, *and he saw* (וַיַּרְא), *and behold* (וְהִנֵּה) Esau was coming, and with him four hundred men. (33:1)

Parallel to the sunlight that shines upon Jacob after wrestling through the night and seeing God face to face is the light of Creation:

> And darkness was upon the face of the deep; and the spirit of God hovered over the face of the waters. And God said: Let there be light. And there was light. And God *saw* (וַיַּרְא) the light that it was good. . . . And God *saw* (וַיַּרְא) everything that He had made, *and behold* (וְהִנֵּה) it was very good. (1:2–4, 31)

The light that shines upon Jacob, after wrestling with the angel at night, is connected to the light of Creation, but this spiritual light brings not a vision of the Divine, but a vision of Esau and his army. Jacob's spiritual light would mean little, if he could not make peace with his brother.

* * *

It is clear that Jacob's very physical struggle with Esau is a spiritual struggle as well. Before Jacob can face Esau, the man, he must wrestle with an angel of God. When he finally does meet his brother, Jacob says, "I have seen your face as one sees the face of God" (33:10). We find this transposition of man and angel when Abraham greets three angels who appear to him as men. The words in the story of Abraham parallel Jacob's encounter with Esau:

ABRAHAM AND THE THREE ANGELS Genesis 18:2–33	JACOB'S ENCOUNTER WITH ESAU Genesis 33:1–16
(וישא עיניו וירא והנה) *And he lifted his eyes and he saw, and, behold,* three men stood over him.	(וישא יעקב עיניו וירא והנה) *And Jacob lifted up his eyes and he saw, and, behold,* Esau was coming, and with him were four hundred men.
And he saw, and he ran toward them from the door of the tent, *and bowed down to the earth* (וישתחו ארצה).	. . . *and he bowed down to the earth* (וישתחו ארצה) seven times, until he came near to his brother.

My lord, if now I have found favor in your eyes (אדני אם־נא מצאתי חן בעיניך),	*. . . if now I have found favor in your eyes* (אם־נא מצאתי חן בעיניך),
please do not pass over from your servant. (אל־נא תעבר מעל עבדך).	*let my lord, please, pass over before his servant.* (יעבר־נא אדני לפני עבדו)
And Abraham *returned* (שׁב) to his place.	And Esau *returned* (וישׁב) on that day on his way toward Seir.

Abraham lifts his eyes and sees angels in the guise of men; Jacob lifts *his* eyes and sees his brother with a threatening entourage of men. Both Abraham and Jacob *bow to the ground* and verbalize the phrase, *if I have found favor in your eyes.* Abraham addresses his guests as *my lords,* and Jacob addresses Esau as *my lord.* Abraham asks his guests, *please do not pass over from your servant.* After Jacob reconciles with Esau, Jacob encourages the departure of his brother saying, *please pass over before his servant.* Abraham returns to his place, and Esau *returns* to Seir.

By the ambiguous identification of man and angel, the Torah is telling us that our work on the human level has spiritual ramifications. Abraham's acts of kindness to three strange men was a service to angels of God. Similarly, Jacob's effort to repair the rift between himself and his brother was a service to God. The message is clear. Our spiritual work and our interactions with other human beings are not separate endeavors. While we live on earth, the spiritual and physical are always interconnected.

Permit me to make a personal digression. When I first discovered the parallels in the chart above, I was troubled. Perhaps the duplication of these words and phrases is governed by the fact that both sections deal with an extraordinary meeting of men (or man and angel). In such cases, one might expect to find phrases such as, *and he bowed down to the earth.* Are the parallels between Jacob's encounter with Esau and Abraham's encounter with the angels intended or fortuitous? If these two sections are really intended to be parallel texts, they should be connected by numerical symmetry. I decided to check the word *and he bowed down* (וישתחו). The Torah doesn't disappoint. The account of Abraham bowing to the earth is the *first* time the exact word, *and he bowed down* (וישתחו), is written in the Torah. The account of Jacob bowing to the earth is the *seventh* time this exact word, וישתחו, is found in the Torah. The numerical symmetry of Abraham and Jacob bowing to the ground confirms the intertextual relationship

וישתחו
and he bowed down
18:2; 19:1; 23:7, 12;
24:26, 52; 33:3

between these two stories. Parallels that were discovered by listening for echoes became corroborated by the binding power of numerical symmetry. Now we can understand the first half of our verse (32:22). Jacob's offering passed over על־פניו, *for the sake of his/His face* – for the sake of the face of his brother, and for the sake of the face of God.

The Darkness Called Night (לילה)

As noted before, the word *night* (לילה) appears in Genesis 32:22 for the *twenty-first* time in the Torah:

> And the offering passed over before him, while he lodged *that night* (בלילה־ההוא) in the camp. (32:22)

It is the *seventh* time *night* (בלילה) appears together with the word *that/ he* (ההוא/הוא). It is also the *seventh* time *night* is written in narratives with Jacob. When we probe the first occurrence of *night* in the Torah, we begin to uncover its symbolic meaning.

The *first* time we find the word *night* is in the account of Day One (in the same paragraph where we find the first *face*):

> The spirit of God hovered over the *face* of (פני) the waters. And God said: Let there be light. And there was light. And God called to the light Day, and to the darkness He called *night* (לילה). (1:5)

Just as the light of Day One is a spiritual light, so, too, is the darkness of Day One a spiritual darkness. The name of this spiritual darkness is *night*. *Night* is the veil that hides God's face, so to speak, and it is this hiddenness of God's presence that is called evil. In man, *night* represents the evil inclination within his heart. It is this *night* with which Jacob struggles, and ultimately subdues. It is during the *night* that Jacob makes his final preparations for the offering that would bring light to the darkness that clouded the first offering. When this preparation is completed, when man reaches perfection in both his man/God and man/man relationships, then *night*, which conceals the light of God, reaches completion, too:

> And the offering passed over before his face, while he lodged *that night* in the camp. (32:22)

After sending his offering ahead to his brother, and wrestling with the angel throughout the night, the sunlight shines with the morning sun:

> Then the sun rose upon him as he passed over *Penuel* (Face of God).
>
> (32:32)

* * *

The "eighth" *night* (3×7th $+ 1$) is found in the verse that immediately follows Genesis 32:22. Jacob wrestles with the angel and sees God face to face, even in the dark of night:

> And he *rose up* (ויקם) on that night (בלילה הוא) [the *eighth* time, also, for the conjuncture of night with ההוא/הוא], and took (ויקח) his two wives (את־שתי נשיו), and his two (ואת־שתי) handmaids, and his eleven children, and passed over the crossing Jabbok. . . . And Jacob was left alone; and a man wrestled with him until the *breaking of the dawn* (עלות השחר). . . . Jacob named the place Peniel, "for I have seen God face to face, yet my life has been preserved."
>
> (32:23–31)

The word *dawn* (שחר) occurs only three times in the Torah: twice in the section above (32:25, 27), and once in the narrative of Sodom and Gomorrah. The words in one place reverberate in the other:

> When *the dawn broke* (השחר עלה), the angels hastened Lot saying: "Arise (קום), take (קח) your wife (את־אשתך), and your two (ואת־שתי) daughters that are found, lest you be swept away in the iniquity of the city."
>
> (19:15)

The *breaking of the dawn* in the Sodom and Gomorrah narrative brought destruction to the outer manifestation of evil that enveloped those cities. The *breaking of the dawn* in the Jacob narrative brings a subjugation of the inner evil that dwells in the heart of man.

There is one other connection between our section on Jacob and the narrative of Sodom and Gomorrah: Both have allusions to messianism. At the end of the Sodom and Gomorrah narrative it is written:

> And they made their father drink wine on that night (בלילה הוא).[87] And the firstborn went in and lay with her father. . . . And the firstborn bore a son, and called his name Moab. . . .
>
> (19:33–37)

Moab is the ancestor of Ruth. Ruth is the great-grandmother of David, from whom will come the Messiah. The dawn in the Jacob narrative, the dawn that comes after that long night of wrestling with the evil inclination, and subduing it, brings the Messianic Day – a day when Jacob and Esau will truly embrace and kiss both physically and spiritually, the day when Jacob will come unto *my lord unto Seir* (33:14). As Rashi comments: "... when will he go? In the days of the Messiah ...." *Night*, then, on the level of the "eighth," is a prelude to the Messianic Day.

Pass Over (עבר) – The Symbol of Transformation

The verb *pass over* (עבר) appears in our verse for the *fourteenth* time in the Torah:

> And the offering *passed over* (ותעבר) before his face, while he lodged that night in the camp. (32:22)

In order to understand the significance of *pass over* in this verse, we need to examine the context of its *first* appearance in the Torah:

> And God remembered Noah, and every living thing, and all the cattle that were with him in the ark; and God caused a wind to *pass over* (ויעבר) the earth, and the waters subsided. (8:1)

The *passing over* of the wind brings an end to the Flood and a new beginning to a transformed earth. *Pass over*, then, in its first appearance in the Torah, is connected to transformation and renewal. At its twice seventh occurrence in the Torah, *pass over* suggests such a metamorphosis, as well. Its meaning in Genesis 32:22 is a transformation of the first offering – ותעבר המנחה, *the offering passed over*. The *offering* that Jacob sends ahead to Esau during that fateful night brings healing to the rift between brothers, making a *tikkun* of the *offerings* of Cain and Abel that had led to fratricide. Not only is *offering* transformed, but so, too, is Jacob, as he ascends to the level of *Israel* during that momentous night.

Pass over (עבר) reaches the level of the "eighth" appearance in the Torah (2 × 7th + 1), in the same verse that *night* reaches its "eighth" (3 × 7th + 1):

> And he rose up *on that night* (בלילה הוא), and he took [his family] and *passed over the crossing* (ויעבר את מעבר), Jabbok. (32:23)

All that belongs to Jacob *passes over the crossing on that night* – his offering, his family, and his possessions – until Jacob is left utterly alone.

> And he took them, and *passed them over* (ויעברם) the stream, and passed over (ויעבר) that which he had. And Jacob was left alone, and a man wrestled with him until the breaking of the dawn.   (32:23–25)

The verb *cross/pass over* (עבר), a verb of transformation, is emphasized in these sentences. When Jacob succeeds in his wrestling at night, in his inner struggle to perfect his relationship with his brother, as well as with God, Jacob merits a new name:

> No longer shall your name be called Jacob, but *Israel*, for you have striven with God and with men, and you have prevailed.   (32:29)

Jacob's *passing over* on the level of the *eighth* leads to an exalted transformation of being. He is told that his name will be Israel, and, after making peace with his brother, he arrives *whole* (שלם)[88] in the city of Shechem (33:18).[89] Rashi comments: "*Whole*: whole in body ... whole in wealth ... whole in Torah . . . ." Jacob, to be known as *Israel*, is the complete human being.

* * *

One other parallel warrants investigation. The first appearance of *pass over* (עבר) in the story of the Flood, connects indirectly to the first appearances of *night* (לילה) in the story of Creation. Many of the same words appear in both places:

THE FLOOD	CREATION
And God remembered Noah, and every living thing ... and God made to **pass over** (ויעבר) a *wind* (רוח) on *the earth* (הארץ), and *the waters* (המים) subsided. And the fountains of the *deep* (תהום) and the windows of the *heavens* (השמים) were stopped; and the rain from the *heavens* (השמים) was abated. (8:1–2)	In the beginning, God created *the heavens* (השמים) and *the earth* (הארץ). And *the earth* (והארץ) was unformed and void, and darkness was upon the face of the *deep* (תהום); and the *spirit* (ורוח) of God hovered over the face of *the waters* (המים). And God said: "Let there be light". . . . And God called the light Day, and the darkness he called **night** (לילה). (1:1–5)

Pass over connects to the Flood, and the Flood connects to Creation.

The theme of *passing over* (עבר), the theme of transformation and renewal that takes place in the Jacob narrative – after he *passes over* the river *crossing* on that *night* (בלילה־ההוא) – is connected to both the theme of *Day One* and the theme of the Flood. *Day One* is the creation of the universe, the transformation of nothing into something, chaos into form. The Flood is a renewal of Creation. Through Jacob, through the nation that is called by his transformed name, *Israel,* will come the fulfillment of that Creation:

> And the LORD shall be king over all the earth: *on that day* (ביום ההוא) the LORD shall be one, and His name one. (Zechariah 14:9)

Jacob's Camp (מחנה)

There is one other word to examine from our verse, and that is *camp* (מחנה), the anagram of *offering* (מנחה). *Camp* is the only word in Genesis 32:22 whose *first* through *eighth* appearances in the Torah all occur within the section dealing with the reconciliation of Jacob and Esau. Let us examine the *first* occurrence of *camp* in order to shed light on its fundamental meaning:

> And Jacob went on his way, and angels of God encountered him. And Jacob said when he saw them: This is a *camp* of (מַחֲנֵה) God. And he called the name of that place *Two Camps* (מַחֲנָיִם). (32:2–3)

According to Hirsch: "Jacob and his family . . . were a temporary camp, in search of God's Presence [Face]. The angels, too, were a camp in search of something. They sought a human community wherein God could dwell on earth. When these two camps met, Jacob named the place *Machanaim*, the two camps - the *camp of Israel*, and the *camp of God*."[90] *Camp*, then, is the place where the human encounters the Divine, and *face* is the interface, the medium through which this encounter takes place.

At the first use of the word *camp*, Jacob encounters the camp of God. By the *seventh*, Jacob has set his own camp in order:

> And the offering passed over before him, while he lodged that night in the *camp* (במחנה). (32:22)

Jacob's *camp*, at its seventh occurrence in the Torah, is complete.

By its *eighth* appearance, *camp* has reached its most exalted level:

And he [Esau] said: What do you mean by *all this camp* (כל־המחנה) which I have met. And he [Jacob] said: To find favor in the eyes of my LORD/lord. (33:8)

Rashi comments that *the camp* (המחנה), according to its plain meaning, refers to the bearers of the offering (מוליכי המנחה), but that according to its Midrashic interpretation, it indicates groups of angels (מלאכים). We can understand the underpinnings of this Midrash if we are sensitive to the words. The first *camp* in the chapter and in the Torah is a *camp of angels of God.* The מלאכים (which can be rendered as *angels* or *messengers*) that Jacob sends ahead to Esau (32:4) are the same ones that Jacob encountered in God's camp (32:2–3). The camp from Jacob that Esau first meets is the group of angels who appear as human "bearers of the offering." Just as *camp* (מחנה) and *offering* (מנחה) are interchangeable in their letters, so too are the human bearers of the offering interchangeable with the angelic camp of God. Jacob's camp had become the Twin Camps (מַחֲנָיִם) of both man and God. When Esau asks, "What do you mean by all this *camp*?", Jacob can respond that the purpose of his *camp*, on the level of the *eighth*, is to find favor in the *eyes of my LORD/lord* - in the *eyes of my God* and in the *eyes of my brother.* Through the righteous conduct of *Jacob's camp*, the *camp of God* can dwell on earth. Indeed, in its wanderings in the wilderness and in its encounter at Sinai, the community of Israel is called *camp*, and Hashem's Presence is with them:

And Moses brought forth the people out of the *camp* (המחנה) to meet with God; and they stood at the nether side of the mount.

(Exodus 19:17)

For the LORD your God walks in the midst of *your camp* (מחנך), to give up your enemies before your face, therefore shall *your camp* (מחניך) be holy. . . . (Deuteronomy 23:15)

* * *

We have explored the extraordinary numerical symmetry of Genesis 32:22. Virtually every word in the verse – offering (מנחה), his face (פניו), night (לילה), the phrase *that night* (לילה הוא/ההוא) *pass over* (עבר), and *camp* (מנחה) – appears there for the seventh or multiple of seventh time in the Torah. In addition to this convergence at their seventh appearance in the Torah, many of the same words are paired together at their first and/ or eighth appearances, as well. *Offering* and *his face* are found together in their first emergence in the Torah. *Offering*'s eighth occurrence is in a verse containing the word *face* (the seventh *face* since 32:22). The "eighth" showings for both *pass over* ($4 \times 7 + 1$) and *night* ($3 \times 7 + 1$) occur in the same verse, and, in addition, these words are connected indirectly in their first appearance. All this is not fortuitous. Not only do all these words connect in their numbers, we have observed that they are linked in an intricate web of meaning and theme.

When I observe the numerical symmetry of this verse, and recall other exquisite symmetries throughout the Torah, I am struck with awe. For Cassuto, numerical symmetry is the "golden thread" that binds the Torah together, providing convincing proof of the unity of the text. And what a beautiful tapestry it is! Every word is connected. Even the counting of letters adds to our esthetic appreciation. But it is more than that. On the face of it, the concept of numerical symmetry is very difficult to accept. Ordinary books are just not written that way. That words should be written in a text in groupings of sevens, with the seventh connected to the first, is highly unlikely, but it is difficult to refute the evidence that stands before us. To accept this evidence is to accept the Divine imprint in the Torah, for no human hand could have written such a text. For me, this "golden thread" that weaves its way through the words and letters of the Torah is an intimation of the presence of God.

* * *

In addition to the esthetic and spiritual reasons sited above, there is a practical purpose for counting words and letters. The observation of numerical symmetries is invaluable to a comprehensive study of the biblical text. Simply by counting words, we can confirm and/or strengthen literary parallels drawn by more conventional methods, as well as draw our attention to new parallels that might otherwise be overlooked. Moreover, counting words in their cycles of sevens, finding other places where the same word may be emphasized seven times, and observing the context of the first, seventh, and eighth can help us uncover the simple meaning of the words in a verse, as well as the deeper meaning of the text as a whole.

The numerical symmetry of Genesis 32:22 teaches us that the *offering* that Jacob sends is more than just a gift to appease Esau. It is a *tikkun*, a repair of the first set of offerings, the *offerings* of Cain and Abel. The *night* when Jacob sends ahead this offering, the same night that he wrestles with the angel, is not just any night: it is *that night*. It is related to the *night* of Day One – to the darkness that hides the face of God hovering over the waters. The *passing over* of this offering, and Jacob's *passing over* the river *crossing* – where he wrestles with this darkness in the human spirit, and prevails – brings as much a transformation to Jacob as the wind that *passed over* the Flood brought to the renewed earth. The *camp* of Jacob reaches the level where it can dwell with the *camp* of God:

ותעבר המנחה על־פניו והוא לן בלילה־ההוא במחנה

And the offering passed over before his face, while he lodged that night in the camp.   (32:22)

One last word. Jacob's *offering* brought him to the level of the *eighth*, the level where he could see God *face to face* (32:31), only because Jacob, unlike Cain and Abel, learned to be sensitive to both the service of God *and* the feelings of his brother. The Torah is teaching us that both our service to God and our treatment of our fellow human beings must be on the most exalted level possible, to the end that we be worthy that *our camp* and *God's camp* can dwell together on earth. Then we will be worthy of the name Israel, for we will have perfected our relationship with both God and man. Then we will become like our father, Israel, as it is written:

... for you have striven with God and with men, and have prevailed.
                                                                (32:29)

Chapter 8

Some Final Observations

I<small>N ORDER TO</small> fully understand any biblical verse, part of the analysis must include sensitivity to the echo that each word brings to that verse from other places in the Torah. The counting of words and letters in their numerical cycles can help us locate parallel verses that add meaning to the text we are studying. Numerical symmetry can work in reverse, as well. Literary parallels that are found by more conventional methods can be strengthened by the discovery of a numerical bond. Numerical symmetry, therefore, can both discover and confirm. Parallels that might otherwise remain hidden are discovered through the searchlight of numerical symmetry. Parallels that are more obvious receive confirmation by the binding strength this symmetry provides.

Full Circle

The first verse of the Torah has twenty-eight (4×7) letters:

בראשית ברא אלקים את השמים ואת הארץ

In the beginning God created the heavens and the earth. (Genesis 1:1)

The last clause of the Torah has twenty-one (3×7) letters:

אשר עשה משה לעיני כל־ישראל

. . . which Moses made before the eyes of all Israel.

(Deuteronomy 34:12)

The letters in the Torah's last clause and first verse total *forty-nine*. This perfect symmetry of seven times seven suggests a connection between the last phrase of the Torah to the first verse of the Torah.

Rashi comments on the first word, בראשית: "Our rabbis have interpreted it: for the sake of the Torah which is called *the beginning of His way* (Proverbs 8:22), and for the sake of Israel, which is called *the beginning of His crops* (Jeremiah 2:3)." According to this Midrashic interpretation, God created the world for ראשית, for the sake of those things that are called *first* – Torah and Israel.

Israel, the last word in the Torah, is followed by בראשית, the first word of the Torah, which according to Rashi and Midrash Rabbah refers to Israel and Torah.

"Moses made," (עשה משה) corresponds to "God created" (ברא אלקים). The purpose of creation is realized through Torah, which Moses made manifest to Israel. This correlation suggests that human contribution (which *Moses made*) is essential to the fulfillment of Creation (which *God created*).[91]

When we read the Torah as a circle, the first verse follows the last: *For the sake of the Torah, which Moses made manifest to the eyes of all Israel, did God create the heavens and the earth.*

A View from Above

We have explored in great detail the extraordinary phenomenon of word patterns in the Torah. We have scrutinized this tree of life leaf by leaf. To appreciate the magnificence of this design, the Torah beckons us to gaze upon these leaves as a whole, to encounter the tree. See the "Words in Sevens" graphic on the following page.

In the very first chapter of the Torah, there are nine words that appear in multiples of seven: *God, earth, saw, good, that, bird, creep, day,* and the word את. Each of these shapes a unit, wherein the *seventh* completes the motif launched by the *first*.

For example, four words reach a count of *seven* in the last verse of Genesis 1, *saw, all, made* and *good*: "And God *saw all* that He had *made*,

WORDS IN SEVENS
Numerical Convergence in Genesis 32:22

Offering – 7th, *camp* – 7th, *pass over* – 14th, *his face* – 7th, *night* – 21st, *that night* – 7th,
The first of each connects to either the *offering* of Cain and the falling of *his face*, the darkness called *night*,
the wind the *passes over* the waters of the Flood, or the *camp* of God.

Numerical Convergence in Gen. 3:6
saw that it was good, tree, *fruit*, *eat/food*

Voice
7 times in *Parashat Toldot*
7 times at Sinai in Exodus
7 times at Sinai in Deuteronomy

Generations of Adam
Man, Elokim, years, create/made

Garden of Eden
Field, make/do, life/beast

All/Every:

Gen. 1: 14 times
Gen. 3: 7 times
Gen. 6: 14 times
Gen. 8: 14 times
Gen. 9: 21 times;
Gen. 11; 14; 19; 20: 7 times each
Gen. 5–12:3: 91 times

Intertextual Connections

Noah's *ark* to the *ark* of baby Moses
After its kind : creation to the Flood
Herbage (עשׂב): Creation to Noah
All (כל): Creation to the Flood to Abraham
Wind : Creation to the Flood
Darkness : Creation to plague of darkness
Tree and *fruit* : Creation to Garden of Eden
Bread: Exile from Eden to *manna* in the desert
Name/there : Generations of Noah to Abraham
Create : Creation to Garden of Eden
Night : Creation to Flood
Dreams : Joseph's dreams to recall of dreams

The Flood (Gen. 6:9–9:17)
Noah, destroy/corrupt, flesh, after its kind, water, all.

Seven Divine communications

Making the Ark (Gen. 6:14–22):
make, ark, enter (בא)

Parashat Noah (Gen. 6:8–11:32):
Hashem, earth, water, Mankind (האדם)

Brother

Cain and Abel (Gen. 4:1–17)
Jacob and Esau (Gen. 25–27)
Jacob and Esau (Gen. 32)
Joseph (Gen. 37; 44; 45; 47)

Protagonists

Names of Patriarchs in Torah: $10^3+10^2+10^1$
Abram/Abraham : 210X in Torah
Isaac/He will laugh : 100X in Torah
Jacob/Israel: 800X in Torah
Cain and Abel: 7X each in story of the brothers
Noah: 28X in Flood
Adam/man: 28X in Gen. 1–4
Names of God: 70X in Gen. 1–4
Elokim : 7X in Gen. 5:1–6:8
Hashem : 7X in Parashat Noah
Hashem in Torah: 7 X 10 X 26

Creation

God, made, earth, saw, all, good, that,
bird/fly, creep, day, את, waters (in Days
2-3), *create* (Gen. 1:1–2:4)

Hashem in Torah: 7 X 10 X 26

Patriarchs in Torah: 1000 + 100 + 10

and, behold, it was very good." The *good* that God *saw* in *all* that He had *made* reached a culmination at the *seven*-count for these words in the same verse.[92]

* * *

Key words that fail to have numerical symmetry based upon seven in the Creation narrative form a numerical pattern over larger or smaller literary units:

Create (ברא) makes its *seventh* appearance at the beginning of the Garden of Eden section: "These are the generations of the heavens and the earth when they were *created* (בהבראם)" (Genesis 2:4).

Night makes its *seventh* appearance at the end of the Noah saga: "Day and *night* shall not cease" (8:22).

made   עשה
1:7, 11, 12, 16, 25, 26, 31

Made is recorded *ten* times in the entire Creation text, three of which are on the Sabbath and *seven* related to physical creation.

All/every is written *seven* times in the six days of creation, and three more times in Day Seven. *All* is written in multiples of sevens in Genesis 1, 3, 6, 8, 9, 14, 19, 20, and 140 times altogether in Genesis 5–22.

* * *

The protagonists in the literary sections of Genesis appear in multiples of seven:

Man/Adam is written *twenty-eight* times in the stories of the first family (1–4), and *fourteen* times in the generations of Man (5:1–6:8).

In the story of Adam and Eve's first two sons (4:1–17), the names of *Cain* and *Abel* recur *seven* times each. Also, their relationship as brothers is emphasized by the *seven*-count of the word *brother*. *Brother* appears in patterns of seven throughout the sibling stories in Genesis: in the account of Cain and Abel, in the saga of Jacob and Esau, and in numerous chapters of the Joseph epic. The phrase *Aaron your brother* recurs *seven* times in the Book of Exodus, concluding the stories of sibling rivalry with sibling harmony. Aaron rejoices at reuniting with his younger brother (Exodus 4:14), and at the *seventh*, Moses is to adorn Aaron and his sons in priestly garments, void of any trace of sibling jealousy: "Put these on *Aaron your brother* and his sons, as well, and anoint them" (28:41).

Noah appears *twenty-eight* times in the story of the Flood (Genesis 6:9–9:17).

The various Names of God reveal powerful numerical symmetries. In the Creation narrative, the five-letter Name, *Elokim* (אלקים), is recorded *thirty-five* times, five times seven. In the ensuing chapters, the accounts of the Garden of Eden and Cain and Abel, we find the four-letter Name, *Hashem* (the LORD), *ten* times, and the combined Name, *Hashem Elokim, ten* more times, with an additional *five* for *Elokim,* making a total for all the various *Names of God,* in the first four chapters of Genesis, *seventy.* In the section of the generations of Man at the end of *Parashat Bereishit* (5:1–6:8), we find *Ekohim seven* more times, and in the entire *Parashat Noah,* Genesis 6:8 through the end of chapter 11, *Hashem* is written *seven* times, again. In the Book of Exodus, *Hashem* occurs *seven* times in the account of the theophany at the burning bush, and *seven* times in Exodus 6. The pattern for *Hashem,* in the first twenty chapters of Exodus is *seven, twice seven squared, sixty, twice seven squared.* (See chart on *Hashem in Exodus.*) In the Torah as a whole, *Hashem* (יהוה), the four-letter Name of the LORD, reveals an amazing count: 26 (the *gematria* of the Name), *times seven times ten,* or $26 \times 7 \times 10$.

The patriarchal names reach sums in the whole of the Torah in patterns of *ten. Abram/Abraham* recurs a total of *210* times in the Torah (a multiple of both ten and seven). The letters that form the name of *Isaac* (יצחק) recur *100* times.[93] *Jacob/Israel* reaches a total of exactly *800.* The total sum for the words that form the names of the *Patriarchs* is *1110,* that is, $10^3 + 10^2 + 10^1$.

The numerical patterns enumerated above defy the theory that the Torah is an amalgam of contradictory documents pasted together by a redactor. Numerical symmetry reveals a unity of text, with all the sections interrelated and forming a dynamic whole. One should not expect to find a numerical pattern for every word, or even most words. But the words that *do* follow these symmetries are not random, and they are more frequent than mere chance would produce. That the names of *Adam, Cain, Abel, Noah, Abram/Abraham, Isaac, Jacob/Israel, Elokim, Hashem,* and *Hashem-Elokim* are all inscribed in perfect numerical harmony cannot be fortuitous. The suggestion that the Torah is an amalgam of different documents written by different authors defies credibility.

* * *

Many key words recur in multiples of *seven* over both small and extended portions of text.

In Genesis 5:1–6:8, which recounts the generations of man up to the Flood, listing the *births, days,* and *years* of *man, who God created,* we find the words of this theme in multiples of *seven,* many of which are clustered at the beginning and end of these passages: *God, created/made, man, birth, days,* and *years.*

Key words related to the great Flood (6:9–9:17) are written in multiples of *seven: Noah, destroy* (שחת), *flesh, after its kind,* and *covenant. God speaks to Noah seven times. Bring/enter* (בוא) is recorded *seven* times in the paragraph relating the entering into the ark. In Genesis 6, the chapter wherein Noah makes the ark, both *make* and *ark* are found *seven* times each.

In *Parashat Noah* as a whole (6:8–11:32), *water,* recurs *twenty-one* times, *Hashem fourteen* times, and the word, *seven, fourteen* times. *Earth* is written *fourteen* times in Chapter 7, *twenty-eight* times in Chapters 8–10, and *forty-nine* times in Chapters 7–11.

The little word *all/every* (כל) moves through the early Genesis stories in cycles of sevens, emphasizing God's role in every detail of His created world. *All/every* is recorded *fourteen* times in the Creation narrative of Genesis 1, *seven* times in the Garden of Eden (Genesis 3), *fourteen* times in in the Flood narrative, in both Genesis 6 and 8, *twenty-one* times in the aftermath of the Flood (Genesis 9), and *140* times from Genesis 5 through 22, culminating with the phrase that God speaks to Abram, "in your seed shall *all* the nations of the earth be blessed" (22:18). In each of these groupings of *all,* there is a relationship between the *seventh* and the *first.*

*   *   *

Throughout this book, we have demonstrated that the *seventh* is related thematically to the *first.* The *first* conveys import to the *seventh.* When the Torah inscribes her words in numerical patterns, she is not just infusing the text with numerical harmony, sewing a golden thread to bind the fabric of Torah. She is repeating these words to direct the student of Torah to relationships between verses, to the growth of these branches that produce leaves of interrelated themes. Let us review a few examples of the interrelationship between the *seventh* and the *first.*

The *seventh* time the word *created* appears in the Torah is in Genesis 2:4, with many of the same words found in 1:1 (*God, create, heavens,* and *earth*), providing evidence to the unity of Genesis 1 and 2, as opposed to those critics who hold these chapters to be two creation stories written by different authors.

"The woman saw that … the *tree* was desirable to make one wise, so she took from its *fruit* and she did eat." (3:6). This verse marks the *seventh* time we find *tree* and *fruit* in the Torah (as well as sevens for *eat/food,* and *saw **that** it was good*). The *first* is when God created *fruit trees* (1:29). This numerical symmetry emphasizes that God had provided many other fruit trees for eating (1:29), but Eve and Adam chose the solitary forbidden tree from among all the other fruit trees that God had created for them to eat: "Every *tree* that has seed-bearing *fruit*; they shall be yours for *eating*" (1:29).

Dreams are a recurring theme in the story of Joseph. *Dream* is written in the Joseph epic for the *first* time in Genesis 37:15, "Joseph *dreamed* a dream, and he told it to his brothers." At the six times *seventh* recurrence of *dream* in this saga, we are reminded of the *first,* "And Joseph remembered the dreams which he had *dreamt*" (42:29). The thread of Joseph's dreams is bound by the link between the *first* and the *last* of this *sevenfold* series.

Herbage (עשׂב) is written for the *first* time when plants are created on Day Three (1:11). The *seventh,* in the story of Noah, reflects back on the first, "Every moving thing that lives shall be food for you; like the green *herbage* (עשׂב) I have given you everything" (9:3).

The *generations of heaven and earth* (2:4) lead to the *seventh* appearance of *generations* in the "*generations* of Isaac, son of Abraham" (25:19), and to the *tenth* at "these are the *generations* of Jacob" (37:2). The symmetry suggests that the *generations of heaven and earth,* which were created with *ten* statements, reach fulfillment through the *generations of the Patriarchs,* whose names in the Torah all have totals that are multiples of *ten.*

The *midrashic* relationship of Esau to the snake of the garden is reinforced by the sevenfold symmetry of *field* (שׂדה). Esau, "the man of the *field*" (28th) is connected to the "snake that was more cunning than all the beasts of the *field*" (1st).

In *Parashat Toldot,* the word *voice* (קול) occurs *seven* times. We find a *seven*-count for *voice* in the revelation at Sinai in both Exodus 19 and Deuteronomy

5. When Rebekah says *hearken to my voice,* her voice is bound to the *Voice* that reverberates from Sinai. When she ensures that her husband eats from Jacob, instead of Esau, she enacts a *tikkun* for the sin of Eve, who gave her husband fruit from the wrong tree. One day the children of Jacob would come to Sinai and partake of the Tree of Life – the Torah.

In Genesis 32:22, "And the offering passed over before his face, while he lodged that night in the camp," we found a remarkable example of numerical convergence. Counting from the beginning of the Torah, almost every word in this verse has a *sevenfold* total, and the *seventh* is informed by the *first.* The seventh *offering* in the Torah, Jacob's tribute to Esau, is linked to the first *offering* of Cain and Abel by theme and numerical symmetry. The first *offering* causes Cain's face to fall, and *his face fell* (ויפלו פניו) (4:6). This also marks the first פניו, *his face,* in the Torah. Jacob hopes to *lift his face* (אולי ישא פני) (32:21) through the seventh *offering* he sends *before his face* (על־פניו). The *offering* is sent at *night,* not any night, but *that night.* The verse marks the twenty-first *night* in the Torah, and the seventh *that night.* The first is the *night* of Day One, the ultimate darkness. The *offering* is sent ahead throughout *that night* (בלילה־ההוא), while Jacob wrestles with the angel who tells Jacob his name will be Israel. Sending an *offering* to make peace with his brother earns Jacob a new name, for he has "striven with God and man, and he has prevailed." The *passing over* of the *offering,* the *fourteenth pass over,* yields as much a transformation to Jacob as the first *pass over,* when God caused a wind to *pass over* the waters to renew the earth that was destroyed in the Flood (8:1). Jacob's *camp,* at the seventh, has become the *twin-camps* of both man and God.

* * *

One approach to numerical symmetry is to count key words within a given literary section and note the relationship between the *seventh* and the *first.* However, there is another approach to studying word patterns. Words in the Torah have a life force of their own, and the *first* and the *seventh* multiple of key words define the literary unit for that word. By following the flow of these verses, we can explore the progressive theme of each of these words, from the *first* to its completion at the *seventh.* For example, *all* moves from *all* the works of creation, to *all* the animals of the ark, to *all* the generations of man, to *all* the families of the earth who will be blessed through Abraham. *Dreams* in the Joseph saga form a literary unit over six chapters, where Joseph recalls the *dream he had dreamt*. The *ark* that saves Noah becomes linked to the *ark* that saves Moses. The first *ark* of this sevenfold unit (Genesis 6:14) preserves the continuity of mankind and all life on earth, and the *last* (Exodus 2:5) saves the man who would bring Torah to Israel and prepare the way for the spiritual salvation of all mankind. Each of these words forms a literary unit based on its numerical symmetry. As we trace the movement of these words through their passages, we gain a comprehensive perspective of the totality these words represent.

Entangled Words

What right do we have to claim that Jacob achieved a *tikkun*, a repair of the offerings of Cain and Abel, or that the *voice* of Rebekah is connected to the *Voice* at Sinai? Does the *ark* of the infant Moses really have any correlation with the *ark* of Noah? Aren't these events separated by time and space?

In the quantum world, a pair of particles can become entangled.[94] Even if two entangled particles become separated by great distances, as far as one galaxy to another, the measurement of the state of one will determine the state of its partner. Einstein called this "spooky action at a distance." Niels Bohr argued that two entangled quantum particles, even if they are far apart in space and time, are complementary and must be regarded as a single quantum system.[95] The laws of classical physics do not determine the correlation between the entangled particles. There are no physical hidden variables that affect the interrelationship of the particles. However, *spiritual* influences can circumvent the limitations of time and space.

Perhaps, words of Torah that are bound in sevens are like entangled particles. As entangled words, the *seventh* and the *first* are interrelated, each affecting the other. The *seventh* can complete the mission of the *first*, or even repair the flaw in the *first*. The spiritual quality of the *first* can resonate in the *seventh*. Entangled particles are correlated with each other, even if separated in space-time. Similarly, sevenfold groups of words correlate with each other, no matter how far apart these words occur within the Torah text.[96]

Therefore, the *offering* of Jacob can repair the *offerings* of Cain and Abel, and the meal that Rebekah prepares for Isaac can become a *tikkun* for the fruit that Eve gives to Adam. To hearken to the *voice* of Rebekah can correlate to the *Voice* that resonates at Sinai, and Jacob's *bowing* before Esau can have a spiritual connection to Abraham *bowing* before angels of God. The *ark* that saves Moses can be a spiritual manifestation of the *ark* that saves Noah, and the *bread* that falls from heaven (Exodus 16:32) can replace the *bread* for which Adam has to labor. Cain and Abel, Jacob and Esau, and Joseph and his siblings, are an entangled relationship of *brothers* that culminates in the peace of Aaron and Moses. The *all* of Creation and the *all* of the Flood lead to the *all* of the blessings that flow through Abraham.

* * *

Umberto Cassuto once wrote that numerical symmetry is the golden thread that binds the Torah together. This thread weaves its way through the Tree of Life, joining the *seventh* to the *first*, interconnecting words and themes across literary sections both large and small, leaving the imprint of God in every textual leaf of this Tree.

Walt Whitman found God within leaves of grass.

> A child said What is the grass? fetching it to me with full hands;
> How could I answer the child? I do not know what it is any more than he.
> I guess it must be the flag of my disposition, out of hopeful green stuff woven.
> Or I guess it is the handkerchief of the LORD,
> A scented gift and remembrancer designedly dropt,
> Bearing the Owner's name someway in the corners, that we may see and remark, and say Whose?[97]

We can find the signature of His Name within the numerical patterns He has implanted in the Tree of Life, His gift of Torah to all of us.

Frequency of Words in the Creation Narrative Genesis 1:1–2:3

T HE CHARTS THAT follow tabulate the frequency of each word in the Creation narrative. Key words appear in *multiples of seven*, either in the Creation section alone, or in a larger literary unit. Seven words from Day One appear a multiple of seven times in the entire Creation section: *God, earth, saw, good, that, day*, and the word את. All the words but one that appear more than thirteen times in the section have frequencies that are a *multiple of seven*.

In the charts that tally every word, the last column is labeled "Comments." This column includes sevens that extend outside the Creation narrative. In these cases, the seventh and the first verses are quoted to confirm the relationship between the two.

Tally of Every Word in Day One

There are seven words in Day One that make a sevenfold appearance in the text of the seven days of Creation (highlighted in bold), as presented in the chart on the following pages.

Word	Frequency of Words of Day One in Creation Text, Genesis 1–2:3	Comments
ראשית Beginning	1 (Gen. 1:1)	
ברא created	6 (Gen. 1:1, 21, 27, 27, 27; 2:3)	**First**: In the beginning God **created** the heavens and the earth. **Seventh**: the generations of the heavens and of the earth when they were **created**. (Gen. 1:1, 21, 27, 27, 27; 2:3, 4)
אלקים God	**35** (Gen. 1:1, 2, 3, 4, 4, 5, 6, 7, 8, 9, 10, 10, 11, 12, 14, 16, 17, 18, 20, 21, 21, 22, 24, 25, 25, 26, 27, 27, 28, 28, 29, 31; 2:2, 3, 3).	
את particle object אתם, אתו him, them	**28** (Gen. 1:1, 1, 4, 7, 16, 16, 16, 16, 17, 21, 21, 21, 22, 22, 25, 25, 25, 27, 27, 27, 28, 28, 29, 29, 30, 31; 2:3, 3)	In Genesis 1, there are seven 22-letter strings forming the word את.
שמים heavens	11 (Gen. 1:1, 8, 9, 14, 15, 17, 20, 26, 28, 30; 2:1)	Heavens are written 10 times in the Six Days, symbolizing the ten *Sefirot* manifest in the physical world.
ארץ earth	**21** (Gen. 1:1, 2, 10, 11, 11, 12, 15, 17, 20, 22, 24, 24, 25, 26, 26, 28, 28, 29, 30, 30; 2:1)	Earth appears 20 times in the Six Days of Creation and one more time (**21st**) in Day Seven.
היה to be, was	27 (Gen. 1:2, 3, 3, 5, 5, 6, 6, 7, 8, 8, 9, 11, 13, 13, 14, 14, 15, 15, 19, 19, 23, 23, 24, 29, 30, 31, 31)	
תהו without form	1 (Gen. 1:2)	
בהו void	1 (Gen. 1:2)	

Word	Frequency of Words of Day One in Creation Text, Genesis 1–2:3	Comments
חשך darkness	4 (Gen. 1:5, 14, 16, 18)	**7 *times*** as חשך (as a noun), from Creation through the Ten Plagues (Gen. 1:2, 4, 5, 18; Ex. 10:21, 21, 22) **First:** "*darkness* **upon** the face of the deep" **Seventh:** "thick *darkness* **upon** all the land of Egypt"
לילה night	4 (Gen. 1:5, 14, 16, 18)	**7 times** from Creation through end of the Flood. (Gen. 1:5, 14, 16, 18; 7:4, 12; 8:22) **First:** "God called the light **Day**, and the darkness he called *Night*." **Seventh:** **Day** and *Night* shall not cease.
על on	12 (Gen. 1:2, 2, 7, 11, 15, 17, 20, 20, 26, 28, 29, 30)	
פני face of	4 (Gen. 1:2, 2, 20, 29)	Exact form of פני **First:** "darkness was upon the *face of* the deep." **Seventh:** "when men began to multiply on the *face of* the earth . . . the sons of rulers saw the daughters of men were fair and they took themselves wives from whomever they chose" (1:2, 2, 20, 29; 2:6; 4:14; 6:1). [The evil of men spread a spiritual darkness upon the face of the earth.]
תהום the deep	1 (Gen. 1:2)	
רוח wind/spirit	1 (Gen. 1:2)	**7 times** **Creation through end of Flood.** (Gen. 1:2; 3:8; 6:3, 17; 7:15, 22; 8:1) **First:** "a *wind* from God moved upon the face of the waters" **Seventh:** "God made a *wind* to pass over the earth, and the waters subsided."
מרחפת	1 (Gen. 1:2)	Appears only one time in Torah

Word	Frequency of Words of Day One in Creation Text, Genesis 1–2:3	Comments
מים waters	11 (Gen. 1:2, 6, 6, 6, 7, 9, 10, 10, 20, 21, 22)	**7 times** in Days 2 and 3: the division of waters and gathering of seas. (Gen. 1:6, 6, 6, 7, 9, 10, 10)
אמר said, saying	11 (Gen. 1:3, 6, 9, 11, 14, 20, 22, 24, 26, 28, 29)	ויאמר אלקים, and God said, 10 times: 10 statements of Creation (Gen. 1:3, 6, 9, 11, 14, 20, 24, 26, 28, 29)
אור מאור light, to light, light bearers	13 (Gen. 1:3, 3, 4, 4, 5, 14, 15, 15, 16, 16, 16, 17, 18)	Light + Day in Day One: **7 times**. Light, to light, light bearers, + stars in Creation text: **14 times** (Gen. 1:3, 3, 4, 4, 5, 14, 15, 15, 16, 16, 16, 16, 17, 18)
וירא and saw	7 (Gen. 1:4, 10, 12, 18, 21, 25, 31)	וירא, in the expression וירא אלקים, occurs **7 times**. (The root ראה is found one more time as ותראה, *and appeared*, in Gen. 1: 9)
כי that	7 (Gen. 1:4, 10, 12, 18, 21, 25; 2:3)	Seventh *saw **that** it was good*: "And the woman *saw **that** the tree was good* for eating" (3:6). In this verse, many of the key expressions appear for a seventh multiple, counting from the beginning of the Torah (*tree, eat/food, fruit, that*, and the expression *saw **that** it was good*.)
טוב good	7 (Gen. 1:4, 10, 12, 18, 21, 25, 31)	
יבדל divided	5 (Gen. 1:4, 6, 7, 14, 18)	
בין between	9 (Gen. 1:4, 4, 6, 7, 7, 14, 14, 18, 18)	First: "God divided **between** the light and between the darkness" Seventh: "to divide between the day and **between** the night"
קרא called	5 (Gen. 1:5, 5, 8, 10, 10)	

Word	Frequency of Words of Day One in Creation Text, Genesis 1–2:3	Comments
ערב evening	**6** (Gen. 1:5, 8, 13, 19, 23, 31)	Evening (6) + Night (4) + darkness (4) = **14**
בקר morning	6 (Gen. 1:5, 8, 13, 19, 23, 31)	
יום day	**14** (Gen. 1:5, 5, 8, 13, 14, 14, 16, 18, 19, 23, 31; 2:2, 2, 3)	
אחד one	2 (Gen. 1:5, 9)	

If we examine the first six days of Creation, we find an interesting numerical symmetry based on the number *ten*. There are three words in this section that are recorded in the Torah ten times, or a multiple of ten. The three words that have tenfold frequencies are: *and He said* (10), *heavens* (10), and *earth* (20). The ten statements of Creation produced the tenfold inscription of heaven and the earth.

There are 32 different words in the text of Day One. When we count the frequency of each of these words in the Creation text (Genesis 1–2:3), we would expect half of them to have a frequency that is a multiple of two – an even-numbered frequency. A third of these words should have frequencies that are multiples of 3 (3, 6, 9, 12, 15 . . .). As the multiples get higher, their frequencies should decrease. This is the case for all numbers except multiples of *seven*. When viewing a frequency graph, *multiples* of *seven* spike sharply above random expectation.

Also, words with smaller frequencies are more numerous than words with higher frequencies. Words with high frequencies for a given text are key words in that text (with the exception of pronouns, etc.). **The most frequent key words in the Creation text appear in multiples of seven.** In Genesis 1–2:3, *God* creates the *earth* in a number of *days*. We should expect the words *God, earth,* and *days* to have a high frequency in this text. The frequencies of each of these words are multiples of *seven*: *God* 35 times, *earth* 21 times, and *day* 14 times. As illustrated in the graphs below, *all the significant words that appear more than thirteen times have a frequency that is a multiple of seven.*

NUMBER OF WORDS IN DAY ONE THAT APPEAR IN THE ENTIRE CREATION TEXT AS A MULTIPLE OF EACH FREQUENCY

F R E Q U E N C Y (vertical axis label)

Frequency	Words
2	9 WORDS
3	7 WORDS
4	5 WORDS
5	3 WORDS
6	4 WORDS
7	**7 WORDS**
8	NONE
9	2 WORDS
10	NONE
11	3 WORDS
12	ONE WORD
13	ONE WORD
14	**2 WORDS**
15	NONE
16	NONE
17	NONE
18	NONE
19	NONE
20	NONE
21	**ONE WORD**
22	NONE
23	NONE
24	NONE
25	NONE
26	NONE
27	ONE WORD
28	**ONE WORD**
29	NONE
30	NONE
31	NONE
32	NONE
33	NONE
34	NONE
35	**ONE WORD**

0 1 2 3 4 5 6 7 8 9 10 11

NUMBER OF WORDS FOUND AS A MULTIPLE OF EACH FREQUENCY

There are 32 different words in Day One. As the frequency increases, the number of words found at those frequencies generally decrease. Instead of a decrease, there is a spike at seven. Almost all the words with the highest counts, have frequencies that are multiples of seven.

Tally of all the words in Days Two through Seven

Word	Frequency in Genesis 1:1–2:3	Comments
רקיע firmament	9 (Gen. 1:6, 7, 7, 7, 8, 14, 15, 17, 20)	These are the only times in the Torah.
בתוך midst	1 (Gen. 1:6)	
עשה made	10 (Gen. 1:7, 11, 12, 16, 25, 26, 31; 2:2, 2, 3)	7 for physical creation (Gen. 1), and three more for the Sabbath (Gen. 2:1–3)
אשר which	12 (Gen. 1:7, 7, 11, 12, 21, 29, 29, 30, 31; 2:2, 2, 3)	
תחת under	2 (Gen. 1:7, 9)	
כן so	6 (Gen. 1:7, 9, 11, 15, 24, 30)	Six times in the expression ויהי־כן, and it was so
שני second	1 (Gen. 1:8)	
מקוה, קוה gather, gathering	2 (Gen. 1:9, 10)	
מקום place	1 (Gen. 1:9)	
יבשה dry land	2 (Gen. 1:9, 10)	
ים sea	4 (Gen. 1:10, 22, 26, 28)	

Word	Frequency in Genesis 1:1–2:3	Comments
תוצא bring forth	2 (Gen. 1:12, 24)	
דשא plant	3 (Gen. 1:11, 11, 12)	
עשׂב grain, herbage	4 (Gen. 1:11, 12, 29, 30)	7 times in Genesis (Gen. 1:11, 12, 29, 30; 2:5; 3:18; 9:3). **First**: And the earth brought forth vegetation, **herbage** yielding seed **Seventh**: as with the green **herbage**, I now give you all.
זרע seed/sowing	10 (Gen. 1:11, 11, 11, 12, 12, 12, 29, 29, 29, 29)	
עץ tree	4 (Gen. 1:11, 12, 29, 29)	**14th** in Torah: "a **tree** to be desired to make one wise" (Gen. 3:6)
פרי fruit	4 (Gen. 1:11, 11, 12, 29)	**Seventh**: "She took of its **fruit** and she ate (Gen. 3:6)
מין kind, species	10 (Gen. 1:11, 12, 12, 21, 21, 24, 24, 25, 25, 25)	7 times in Noah (Gen. 6:20, 20, 20; 7:14, 14, 14, 14)
בו in it	4 (Gen. 1:11, 12, 30; 2:3)	
שׁלישׁי third	1 (Gen. 1:13)	
אות sign	1 (Gen. 1:14)	
מועדים seasons	1 (Gen. 1:14)	

Word	Frequency in Genesis 1:1–2:3	Comments
שנים years	1 (Gen. 1:14)	
גדל great	3 (Gen. 1:16, 16, 21)	
ממשלת dominate	3 (Gen. 1:16, 16, 18)	
קטן small	1 (Gen. 1:16)	
כוכבים stars	1 (Gen. 1:16)	
נתן give	2 (Gen. 1:17, 29)	
רביעי fourth	1 (Gen. 1:19)	
שרץ swarm	3 (Gen. 1:20, 20, 21)	7 times in Genesis (Creation through Noah) (Gen. 1:20, 20, 21; 7:21, 21; 8:17; 9:7)
נפש being, creature, animal soul	4 (Gen. 1:20, 21, 24, 30)	
חיה, חית living, life, beast	8 (Gen. 1:20, 21, 24, 24, 25, 28, 30, 30)	22 times in Genesis 1–3 22nd: "to guard the way to the tree of **life** [Torah]," correspond- ing to the 22 letters found in the *Torah*.
עופף, עוף winged creature, fly	7 (Gen. 1:20, 20, 21, 22, 26, 28, 30)	

Word	Frequency in Genesis 1:1–2:3	Comments
תנינם sea monsters	1 (Gen. 1:21)	
כל all, every	17 (Gen. 1:21, 21, 25, 26, 26, 28, 29, 29, 29, 30, 30, 30, 30, 31; 2:1, 2, 3)	14 times in Genesis 1, regarding the creation of **all** the creatures plus 3 more times in the Sabbath.
רמש crawl, crawl- ing thing	7 (Gen. 1:21, 24, 25, 26, 26, 28, 30)	
ברך blessed	3 (Gen. 1:22, 28; 2:3)	
פרו be fruitful	2 (Gen. 1:22, 28)	
רבה multiply	3 (Gen. 1:22, 22, 28)	
מלא fill	2 (Gen. 1:22, 28)	
חמישי fifth	1 (Gen. 1:23)	
בהמה beast, cattle	3 (Gen. 1:24, 25, 26)	
אדם man	2 (Gen. 1:26, 27)	
צלם image	3 (Gen. 1:26, 27, 27)	
דמות likeness	1 (Gen. 1:26)	
רדה rule	2 (Gen. 1:26,28)	

Word	Frequency in Genesis 1:1–2:3	Comments
דג fish	2 (Gen. 1:26, 28)	
זכר male	1 (Gen. 1:27)	
נקבה female	1 (Gen. 1:27)	
כבש subdue	1 (Gen. 1:28)	
לכם to you	1 (Gen. 1:29)	
אכלה food	2 (Gen. 1:29, 30)	
ירק green	1 (Gen. 1:30)	
מאד very	1 (Gen. 1:31)	
ששי sixth	1 (Gen. 1:31)	
כלה completed	2 (Gen. 2:1, 2)	
צבא host	1 (Gen. 2:1)	
שביעי seventh	3 (Gen. 2:2, 2, 3)	
מלאכה work	3 (Gen. 2:2, 2, 3)	

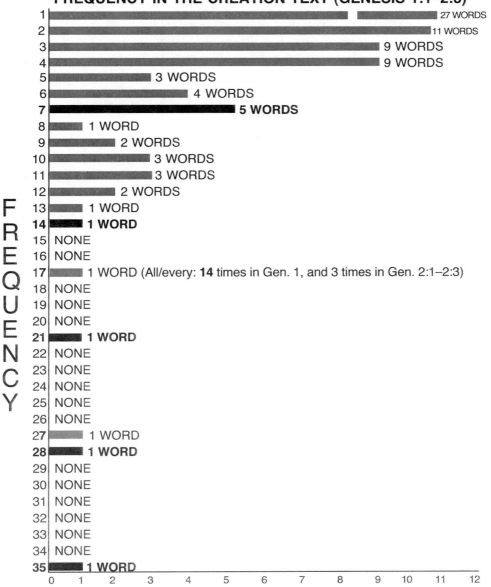

NUMBER OF WORDS THAT APPEAR AT EACH EXACT FREQUENCY IN THE CREATION TEXT (GENESIS 1:1–2:3)

FREQUENCY	
1	27 WORDS
2	11 WORDS
3	9 WORDS
4	9 WORDS
5	3 WORDS
6	4 WORDS
7	**5 WORDS**
8	1 WORD
9	2 WORDS
10	3 WORDS
11	3 WORDS
12	2 WORDS
13	1 WORD
14	**1 WORD**
15	NONE
16	NONE
17	1 WORD (All/every: **14** times in Gen. 1, and 3 times in Gen. 2:1–2:3)
18	NONE
19	NONE
20	NONE
21	**1 WORD**
22	NONE
23	NONE
24	NONE
25	NONE
26	NONE
27	1 WORD
28	**1 WORD**
29	NONE
30	NONE
31	NONE
32	NONE
33	NONE
34	NONE
35	**1 WORD**

NUMBER OF WORDS FOUND AT EACH EXACT FREQUENCY

In the entire Creation text, 27 words appear only once, and 11 words twice. Nine words appear 3 times or 4 times. Three words appear 5 times. As the frequencies increase, the number of words appearing at each frequency decreases. Again, there is a spike at 7. Words with the highest frequencies most often have a *sevenfold* frequency. The words that have a frequency greater than 13 are either multiples of 7, or a multiple of *10* supplemented by an additional 7, as presented in the chart on the previous page.

See the chart on the facing page. There are 88 different words in the Creation text. Therefore, 88 words have a frequency that is a *multiple* of 1. Thirty-two words have a frequency that is a multiple of 2, and 19 words as a multiple of 3. As the multiples decrease, the number of words at those multiples decrease. But there is a spike at 7. Nine words have a frequency of 7, or a *multiple of* 7. All the words that have frequencies that are greater than 13 are either multiples of 7, or a decimal number plus 7.

Furthermore, many of the words in the Creation text that do not have a symmetry based on *seven*, do have a meaningful symmetry over larger textual units. These words form concentric circles of various intertextual units, linking the context of the *seventh* to the theme of the *first*. Below are a few examples of seven-symmetries that extend beyond the account of Creation.

Night (לילה) only occurs four times in the Creation narrative. The *seventh night* in the Torah is connected to the *first*.

First: God called the light *day* (יום), and the darkness He called **night** (לילה).
(Genesis 1:5)

Seventh: So long as the earth endures, seedtime and harvest, cold and heat, summer and winter, *and day* (ויום) *and* **night** (ולילה) shall not cease.
(8:22)

After the Flood, Creation was renewed. The regularity of day and *night* which began on the first day would not be disturbed again.

* * *

NUMBER OF WORDS THAT APPEAR AS A MULTIPLE OF EACH FREQUENCY IN THE CREATION TEXT (GENESIS 1:1–2:3)

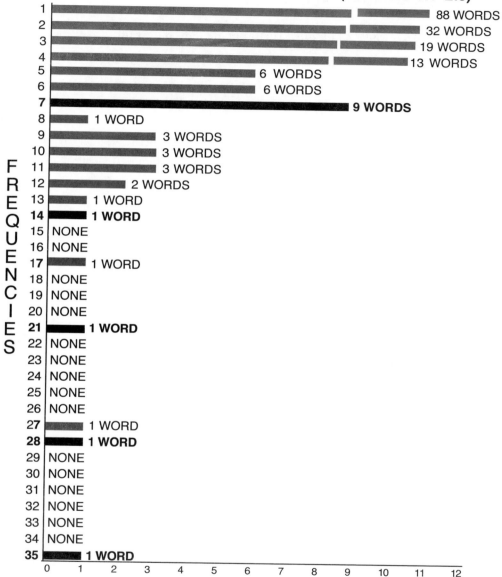

FREQUENCIES

Frequency	Number of Words
1	88 WORDS
2	32 WORDS
3	19 WORDS
4	13 WORDS
5	6 WORDS
6	6 WORDS
7	9 WORDS
8	1 WORD
9	3 WORDS
10	3 WORDS
11	3 WORDS
12	2 WORDS
13	1 WORD
14	1 WORD
15	NONE
16	NONE
17	1 WORD
18	NONE
19	NONE
20	NONE
21	1 WORD
22	NONE
23	NONE
24	NONE
25	NONE
26	NONE
27	1 WORD
28	1 WORD
29	NONE
30	NONE
31	NONE
32	NONE
33	NONE
34	NONE
35	1 WORD

0 1 2 3 4 5 6 7 8 9 10 11 12

NUMBER OF WORDS FOUND AS A MULTIPLE OF EACH FREQUENCY

In the creation text, nine words have a frequency of seven, or a multiple of seven. All the words that have frequencies greater than thirteen are either a multiple of seven, or a multiple of ten plus seven.

Wind/spirit (רוח) occurs only once in our section, but the *seventh* is very much connected to the *first*:

First: And a ***wind/spirit*** (ורוח) of God moved over the face of the waters. (Gen. 1:2)

Seventh: God caused a ***wind/spirit*** (רוח) to pass over the earth, and the waters subsided. (Gen. 8:1)

The *wind/spirit* of God vivified the earth during the original Creation. At its seventh appearance, the *wind/spirit* of God renewed Creation after the Flood.

* * *

The word *herbage* (עשב) appears *seven* times in the Book of Genesis, and the *seventh* reflects the *first*.

First: Let the earth sprout ***herbage***, seed-bearing plants, fruit trees of every kind. . . . (1:11)

Seventh: Every creature that lives shall be yours to eat; as with the green ***herbage***, I give you all these. (9:3)

The textual context and the corresponding numerical symmetry point us back from Noah to the creation of vegetation. Man could now eat meat, like the green *herbage* that was created on Day Three.

* * *

The words *tree* and *fruit* appear together in their *first* and *twice seventh* appearances in the Torah.

First: Let the earth sprout vegetation: seed-bearing plants, ***fruit trees*** of every kind. (1:11)

Fourteenth: The ***tree*** [*twice seventh*] was desirable to make one wise, and she took of its ***fruit*** [*seventh*] and she ate. (3:6)

As discussed earlier, there are a few other words within the Creation text that make a sevenfold appearance in Genesis 3:6: *eat/food*, and the expression *saw … that* it *was good.* They all make their seventh appearance, or multiple thereof, in a verse that is the turning point in the chronicle of Man (Gen. 3:6).

* * *

In addition to the numerical symmetry based on the number *seven,* we can discern symmetries based on the *sexagesimal* and *decimal* systems.

Six words appear either *six* times or twelve times: *created, on, which, evening, morning,* and the expression, *and it was so.* The *six* paragraphs of the *six* days of physical creation end with the *sixfold* refrain: *and there was evening, and there was morning.* God's commands to create are followed by the *sixfold* refrain, *and it was so.* The word *create* appears *six* times, and the *seventh* joins the text of Creation to the Garden of Eden narrative.

Symmetries of *ten* are reflected in the following words and phrases. *Heaven* appears *ten* times in the six-day narrative, making an additional appearance on the Seventh Day. *God speaks ten* times in the tenfold refrain, *and God said.* In Days Two and Three, the section that tells of the division of the waters and the gathering of the seas, *water* is written *ten* times. *Seed* and *species* are found *ten* times each. The word *made* appears *ten* times in the seven days of Creation (*seven* times in the account of the six days, and *three* more in the Sabbath day narrative).

In our examination of the Creation text, we found that the most frequent words have a symmetry based on *seven.* These words express the theme of the section. Symmetries based on seven were found in larger literary units, connecting the context of the seventh to the theme of the first. We were also able to discern symmetries based on *sixes* and *tens.* The Torah text is carefully constructed. Numerical symmetries suggest a unity to the text and provide an aide to revealing relationships between the *first* and the *seventh.*

As this study of the words in the Creation narrative demonstrates, not every word is a multiple of seven. However, the frequency of sevenfold repetitions occurs more than random chance would produce. When the Torah inscribes a word in a given textual section seven times, or a multiple of seven, it is not fortuitous. The Torah wants us to connect the *seventh* to the *first,* and to see the text bracketed by this seventh-first pair as a thematic unit.

Appendix 2

Summary of Words Appearing in Multiples of Seven

Creation (Genesis 1:1–2:3):
    God (אלקים) – 35 times
    Created (ברא) – 7 times in Genesis 1:1–1:4
    את – 28 times
    Earth (ארץ) – 21 times
    Darkness (חשך) – 7 times from Genesis 1:2 – Exodus 10:22
    Face of (פני) – 7 times from Genesis 1:2–6:1
    Wind/spirit (רוח) – 7 times Genesis 1:2–8:1
    Water (מים) – 7 times in Days Two and Three
    and God saw that [it was] good (וירא אלקים ... טוב) – 7 times
    Day (יום) – 14 times
    Made (עשה) – 7 times in Days One through Six, and 3 more in Day Seven
    Grain, herbage (עשב) – 7 times in Genesis; 7th in 9:3
    Tree (עץ) – 14 times in Genesis 1:11–3:6
    Fruit (פרי) – 14 times in Genesis 1:11–3:6
    Swarm (שרץ) – 7 times in Creation through Noah (Genesis 1:20–9:7)
    Winged creature/fly (עופף/עוף) – 7 times
    all/every (כל) – 14 times

Garden of Eden (Genesis. 2:4–3:24):
    Field (שדה) – 7 times
    Make/do (עשה) – 7 times
    Life/beast (חי/חיה) – 14 times
    Man/woman (איש/אשה) – 21 times
    Man/ground (אדם/אדמה) – 21 times in Genesis 2, and 35 times in Genesis 1–3
    Bread (לחם) – 35 times from Genesis 3:19–Exodus 16:32
    Ground (אדמה) – 14 times in Genesis 2:5–4:14
    All (כל) – 7 times in Genesis 3

Cain and Abel (Genesis 4):
    Cain (קין) – 7 times
    Abel (הבל) – 7 times
    Brother (אח) – 7 times

Divine Names:
    Creation – 35 times (Genesis 1:1–2:3)
    Garden of Eden and the family of Adam – 35 times (Genesis 2:4–4:26)
    The Divine Names found in Genesis 1–4 – total 70.

The Generations of Adam (Genesis 5:1–6:8):
    Man (אדם) – 7 times
    God/rulers (אלקים) – 7 times
    Years (שנה) – 49 times
    Created/made (עשה/ברא) – 7 times in total

The Flood (Genesis 6:9–9:17):
    Noah – 28 times in the section (Genesis 6:9–9:17), and 35 times in all of
        Genesis 6–9, which includes prelude and aftermath of the Flood
    Destroy (שחת) – 7 times
    Flesh (בשר) – 14 times

    The Making of the Ark (Genesis 6:14–22):
      Make (עשה) – 7 times
      Ark (תבה) – 7 times
    Come/bring/enter (בוא) – 7 times in Genesis 7, which tells of entering the
        ark
    Specie (after its kind) (מין) – 7 times
    Water (מים) – 21 times
    Flood (מבול) – 7 times in Genesis 6:17–9:11, the first and seventh forming an
        inverse parallel
    Covenant (ברית) – 7 times, all in Genesis 9
    All (כל) – 7 times in Genesis 6; 14 times in Genesis 8; 21 times in Genesis 9
    7 **Divine communications** with Noah

Parashat Noah as a Whole (Genesis 6:8–11:32)
    Earth (ארץ) – 7 times in Genesis 7; 28 times in Genesis 8–10; 49 times in
        Genesis 7–11
    Water (מים) – 21 times
    Hashem (י־הוה) – 14 times: 7 times with Noah, and 7 times with Nimrod
        and the tower
    Mankind (האדם) – 14 times in Genesis 6–11

Sevens that connect Parashat Noah to Other Parts
of the Torah:
    Ark (תבה) – 28 times: Noah's ark to the ark for the infant Moses
    Species (after its kind) (מין) – 7 times for animals In Genesis 1; 7 times for
        animals on the ark in Genesis 6–7

Herbage (עשׂב) – 7 times in Genesis, connecting the creation of plants for eating to the addition of meat after the Flood (first, Genesis 1:11; seventh, Genesis 9:3)

Name (שם) – 7 times in the generations of Noah (Genesis 10), 7 times in times in the story of Babel (Genesis 11:1–9), and 7 times from the Generations of Shem to the blessing of Abram (Genesis 11:10–12:2).

All (כל) – 70 times from beginning of Genesis 6 through end of the Flood (Genesis 9:17); 7 times in Genesis 11; 91 times (13×7) in Genesis 5–12:3; 140 times in Genesis 5–22

Brother in Genesis:

7 times in Genesis 4
14 times in story of Jacob and Esau in *Parashat Toldot*
7 times in story of Jacob and Esau in *Parashat Vayishlach*
7 times in Genesis 31, when Laban and his kinsmen pursue Jacob
21 times in selling of Joseph (Genesis 37)
7 times in Genesis 44
14 times in Genesis 45
7 times in Genesis 47
The phrase *Aaron your brother* – 7 times in Book of Exodus

Patriarchs in multiples of ten:

Isaac/He will laugh – 100 times
Jacob/Israel – 800 times
Abram/Abraham – 210 times (70×3)
Total for patriarchal words: $1110 = 10^3 + 10^2 + 10^1$
(In many individual sections, not listed in this book, the Patriarchs are written in sevens.)

Hashem in the Torah:

1820 times, which equals $7 \times 26 \times 10$

Voice (קול):

7 times in *Parashat Toldot*
7 times in the revelation at Sinai in Exodus
7 times in the revelation at Sinai in Deuteronomy

Numerical Convergence in Genesis 32:22:

Offering (מנחה) 7th
Camp (מחנה) 7th
Pass/cross over (עבר) 14th
His face (פניו) 7th
Night (לילה) 21st
That night (לילה ההוא, לילה הוא) 7th

Notes

1 Translation adapted from Rabbi Dr. H. Freedman, Hebrew-English Edition of the *Babylonian Talmud: Kiddushin* (London: Soncino Press, 1977). The Gemara does not give the result of their counting. (Computer counts do not confirm this identification of the middle words or the middle letter of the Torah.) The margins of the Masoretic text note numerous counts of rare words within the entire Hebrew Bible, and the *Baal HaTurim* notes connections between the contexts of these words. See also *Chagigah* 15b: ". . . they would count all the letters in the Torah."

2 Chanukah occurs on the 25th day of the month of Kislev. The 25th word of the Torah is "light."

3 See *Midrash Rabah* 21, and Eliyahu Kitov, *The Book of Our Heritage, First Volume,* (Jerusalem, New York: Feldheim Publishers, 1978), 210.

4 Num. 31:5.

5 Chief Rabbi of Florence from 1914 to 1925, and professor of Bible at the Hebrew University of Jerusalem.

6 This verse was pointed out to me by a friend and physicist, Larry Polsky. He noted that on a clear night, the maximum number of visible stars are only two to three thousand. Surely Abraham's blessing of progeny was more than that. Telescopes reveal many trillions of stars, but it takes human effort to count them. Similarly, the counting of words in the Torah takes perseverance.

7 Counting of words and letters in this book are counts from the Hebrew Masoretic text.

8 See U. Cassuto, *A Commentary on the Book of Genesis, Part I, From Adam to Noah,* [English Edition], (Jerusalem: Magnes Press, 1961).

9 All counting of words in this book is done in Hebrew, counting Hebrew roots for each word, unless otherwise specified.

10 I have highlighted the English phrases that correspond to the Hebrew words so that the reader can see the seven-word count in English. Each highlighted word

or phrase corresponds to one Hebrew word.

11 A few of Cassuto's counts were in error, and these have been omitted.

12 The Aish HaTorah *Discovery* booklet notes that Professor Ivan Panin discovered over 50 patterns of the number seven in the first verse of the Torah, including the one that we noted.

13 U. Cassuto, *op. cit.*, 15. See App. 1 for an account of every word in the Creation text.

14 See *Tanya, Likutei Amarim*, Chap. 4.

that כי
Gen. 1:4, 10, 12, 18, 21, 25; 2:3, 5, 17, 23; 3:1, 5, 5, 6

15 This marks the fourteenth time the word *that* (כי) occurs in the Torah.

16 The word ברא, *create*, is written fourteen times in the Torah. The first and seventh reflect on each other, "*created* the *heavens* and the *earth*" (Gen. 1:1), and "the *heavens* and the *earth* when they were *created*" (2:4). The next seven also correlate. Eighth: "This is the book of the generations of Adam, in the day *God created man*" (5:1). Fourteenth: "You have but to inquire about bygone ages that came before you, ever since *God created man* on *earth*, from one end of *heaven* to the other..." (Deut. 4:32).

create ברא
Gen. 1:1, 21, 27, 27, 27; 2:3, 4; 5:1, 2, 2; 6:7; Ex. 34:10; Num. 16:30; Deut. 4:32

17 See Cassuto, *op. cit.*, for his commentary on Gen. 2:5 and 3:18.

18 "She is a tree of life to them that lay hold upon her" (Prov. 3:18). When Moses came down from the mount, the people had tasted from the sin of idolatry, and were threatened with death: "Let Me alone ... that I may consume them" (Ex. 32:10), which corresponds to "in the day you eat thereof you shall surely die" (Gen. 2:17).

19 With the birth of Cain's son, Gen. 4:17 marks the end of the story of the life of Cain.

20 There are two other verses with the name of *Cain* in Gen. 4 (4:24, 25), but they are not about the story of Cain's life.

21 The first *bearing* is the *birth* of Cain (Gen. 4:1), where it is written, "Now, the man knew his wife Eve, and she conceived and *bore* Cain, saying, 'I have gained a male child with the LORD.'" In the first *birth*, the LORD is partner with Eve. By the forty-second *birth*, daughters are *born*, who are taken by the sons of *elohim*.

22 See U. Cassuto, *A Commentary on the Book of Genesis, Part II, From Noah to Abraham* [English Edition], (Jerusalem: Magnes Press, 1964), 3.

23 These verses incorporate the narrative of the Flood. Gen. 6:9 begins the story of Noah and the Flood. V. 9:17 concludes the account of the rainbow covenant. The next verse, 9:18, begins a new section – the story of Noah's children and the aftermath of the Flood.

covenant ברית
Gen. 15:18; 17:2, 4, 7, 7, 9, 10, 11, 13, 13, 14, 19, 19, 21

24 *Covenant* appears *fourteen* times in relation to God's covenant with Abraham.

25 The first of the fourteen appearances of *all* in Genesis 8, which describes the end of the Flood and the saving of *all* the animals on the ark.

26 Spelled with a final *tzadee*. *Earth/land* appears three more times as ארצתם, denoting specific portions of land (Gen. 10:5, 20, 31), but not the whole earth, and once as ארצה (11:31).

27 The Torah has designated a smaller literary framework wherein the *seventh* *flood* in the Torah forms a nexus to the *first* (Gen. 6:17; 7:6, 7, 10, 17; 9:11,11):

First: And behold, I do bring the **Flood**-*waters* upon the *earth* – to *destroy all flesh* under the heavens in which there is breath of life. (6:17).

Seventh: I will maintain My covenant with you: never again shall *all flesh* be cut off by the *waters* of a **flood**, and never again shall there be a Flood to *destroy* the *earth*" (9:11). (*Flood* is written twice in 9:11, the first of which is the seventh in the Torah.)

We find the *waters*, *destroy*, *earth*, and *all flesh* together with the *first, sixth* and the *seventh* appearances of *flood* in the Torah. The *first* pronounces the decree, and the *seventh* establishes the covenant that guarantees that never again would there be *floodwaters* to *destroy all flesh* upon the *earth*.

28 God, אלקים, is written twenty times in Gen. 6–11, *seven* times in Gen. 6.

29 U. Cassuto, *op. cit.*, 59.

30 The numerical symmetry of the word שם was taught to me by Rabbi Murray Schaum.

31 In Gen. 10–11, *birth/begat* appears for total of 36 (6 × 6) times, a perfect sexagesimal number, in accord with the culture of Babylon.

32 *All/every* is written 21 times in Gen. 9. The *first* and *seventh* כל modifies the word *beast*. **First**: "The fear of you and the dread of you shall be upon **every beast** of the earth" (9:2). **Seventh**: "at the hand of **every beast** will I require it" (9:5). Both indicate the supremacy of Man over *every beast*. If a beast fails to fear man and kills a man, the beast is put to death (Ex. 21:28).

33 This verse marks the *tenth* appearance of אדמה, when we begin our count from the original curse of the ground in the story of Adam in the garden, where it is written, *cursed is the **ground** because of you*.

34 From the Decalogue to the end of the Book of Exodus, Chaps. 20 through 40, דבר is written fifty times, supplemented by an additional seven.

35 Only the *exact* name and spelling of Israel, ישׂראל, is counted, as we did with Isaac, יצחק. Israelite (f) (ישׂראלית), or Israeli (m) (ישׂראלי) are not included, which are found only in Lev. 24:10–11 (four times total in the Torah for both altogether). "Children of Israel" and even verses such as "Hear O Israel" refer to the progeny of the Patriarch. *Israeli* and *Israelite* refer to the nation of Israel and is one step removed from the Patriarch himself, whereas "children of Israel" bears the Patriarch's name directly.

36 The precise grammatical form of the Hebrew word *knows* (יֹדֵעַ), with the same spelling and vowel points, appears here for the *second* time in the Torah. The *first* time is in the cunning mouth of the Snake: "For God *knows* (ידע) that in the day you eat thereof your eyes shall be opened; you shall be like God, knowing good and evil" (Gen. 3:5).

37 See Rashi to Gen. 3:7: "Even the blind knows when he is naked! What then is *and they knew that they were naked?* One mitzvah was put in their hands, and they stripped themselves of it."

God אלקים
6:2, 4, 9, 11, 12, 13, 22; 7:9, 16; 8:1, 1, 15; 9:1, 6, 8, 12, 16, 17, 26, 27

birth/begat
10:1, 8, 13, 15, 21, 24, 24, 25, 26; 11:10, 11, 11, 12, 13, 13, 14, 15, 15, 16, 17, 17, 18, 19, 19, 20, 21, 21, 22, 23, 23, 24, 25, 25, 26, 27, 27

all/every
9:2, 2, 2, 2, 3, 3, 5, 10, 10, 10, 10, 11, 12, 15, 15, 15, 16, 16, 17, 19, 29

ground אדמה
Gen. 3:17, 19, 23; 4:2, 3, 10, 11, 12, 14; 5:29

38 The term for "permissible cunning" is מרמה; the term for "malicious cunning" is ערמא (*Midrash HaBiur*). See *ArtScroll Tenach Series, Bereishis/Genesis, Vol. 3*, 1150. Rabbi Menachem M. Schneerson notes: "The aspects mentioned in the blessings came about through *mirma* (cunning), for these aspects constitute the sparks of holiness which have fallen to the lowly levels because of 'the serpent [which] was subtle [cunning]' etc. The restoration of these sparks to the realm of holiness, therefore, had to be likewise by means of *mirma*," M. Schneerson, *Likkutei Sichos, Vol. I: Bereishit* [English edition], (Brooklyn: Kehot Publication Society, 1980), 104.

39 Rashi comments on Gen. 27:15: "which he coveted from Nimrod." "According to the *Midrash*, Esau's garments were the very garments that God had originally made for Adam. The garments were passed down through the generations to Nimrod, and Esau took the garments and killed Nimrod in a duel." See *ArtScroll Tenach Series, Bereishis/Genesis, Vol. 1*, 136, 318, *Vol. 3*, 1063; *Sefer HaYashar* 7:24; *Tora Shelema* 3:184.

eat אכל
Gen. 1:29, 30; 2:9, 16, 16, 17, 17; 3:1, 2, 3, 5, 6, 6, 6

40 This marks the *seventh* time the root of the word *eat* (אכל) appears in Chap. 3, and the *fourteenth* in the Torah.

41 How was Isaac able to recognize the smell of Eden? We should consider the Midrash, which says that after the binding of Isaac, God took Isaac into the Garden of Eden, where he stayed for three years (*Bereshis Rabba* 56:11).

42 Threefold repetition is for emphasis. See U. Cassuto, *A Commentary on the Book of Genesis, Part I* (Jerusalem: Magnes Press, 1944 [first English edition, 1961]), 193.

hear שמע
27:5, 6, 8, 13, 34, 43; 28:7

43 *Hear* (שמע) appears for an eighth time in *Parashat Toldot* in Gen. 28:7, "And Jacob hearkened (וישמע) to his father and mother and went to *Paddan-Aram*." In the story of Jacob and Esau and their conflict over the blessings, *hear* (שמע) appears *seven* times.

44 Rashi addresses the plural: "and my *Torahs* – to include the Oral Law, the laws revealed to Moses on Sinai."

voice קול
Gen. 26:5; 27:8, 13, 22, 22, 38, 43

45 In addition to the three verses in Gen. 27, *hear* and *voice* are written together one more time in *Parashat Toldot*: "Because Abraham *hearkened* to My *voice* and kept My charge, My commandments, My statutes, and My Torahs" (26:5). This first recording of *hear* and voice in the *parashah* fixes the essential spirituality of the expression *hearken to my voice*. The word *voice* (קול) appears *seven* times in the *parashah* altogether, forming a complete unit. (The root of the word *hear* (שמע) appears *seven* times in the parts of *Parashat Toldot* that deal with Jacob and Esau.)

hear שמע
27:5, 6, 8, 13, 34, 43; 28:7

46 It is noteworthy that Cain's exile is also to the east (Gen. 4:16). At the *seventh east* in the Torah, Abraham builds an alter to the LORD *east* of Bethel, ". . . with Bethel on the west and Ai on the *east*; and he built there an altar to the LORD and invoked the LORD by name" (12:8).

47 See Malbim to Gen. 3:19. Also, see Zvi Faier's n. 471 to his English translation, *Malbim, Commentary on the Torah, Book One, Beginning and Upheaval* (Jerusalem: Hillel Press, 1978), 280–281.

48 See *Bereishit Rabba* (69:61).

49 Note: *because, heel,* and *Jacob* have the same root, עקב.

50 Some Bibles list Deut. 5:19 as Deut. 5:22.

51 "*I heard your father speaking* (מדבר)" (Gen. 27:6). The word *speaking*, in the form מדבר, appears only four times in the Torah: Gen. 27:6; 29:9; Deut. 4:33; 5:23. Gen. 27:6 and the two verses in Deuteronomy are the only verses in the Torah having both a word from the stem *hear* (שמע) and this exact form of the word *speaking* (מדבר). Both verses in Deuteronomy describe the revelation at Sinai through the aspect of *hearing* the *voice* of God *speaking*: "Did ever a people *hear* (שמע) the *voice* of God *speaking* (מדבר) from the midst of the fire, as you have *heard* (שמע) and live?" (Deut. 4:33); and the related verse, "For who of all flesh has *heard* (שמע) the *voice* of the living God *speaking* (מדבר) from the midst of the fire, as we have, and lived?" (Deut. 5:23). (We should also note that the paragraph wherein this last verse appears [Deut. 5:19–6:3] contains many words that are written in the account of the Garden of Eden.) The juxtaposition of the words *speaking* (מדבר) and *hear* (שמע) in both the narrative of Rebekah and her sons, and in the account of the revelation at Sinai may not be fortuitous. The Torah may be hinting that God wanted Rebekah to overhear Isaac *speaking* with Esau so that Rebekah could intervene in some way. Only the progeny of Jacob could stand at Sinai and "*hear* the voice of God *speaking* from the midst of the fire."

52 The first two relate to the Oral Torah: "Now *hearken to my voice* ... you be for the people before God, that you may bring the matters to God. And you shall teach them the statutes and the laws, and you shall make known to them the way in which they must walk ... and you shall place over them rulers of thousands, rulers of hundreds [etc.] ... and Moses *hearkened to the voice* of his father-in-law, and did all that he had said" (Ex. 18:19–24). The third coupling of *hear* and *voice*, in *Parashat Yitro*, occurs at the making of the covenant between God and His people at Sinai: "And now, if you will indeed *hearken to my Voice*, and you will keep my covenant, then you shall be a precious treasure to Me from among all the peoples ..." (19:3–5). (In the account of the revelation at Sinai in Deuteronomy, the words *hear* and *voice* appear together ten times.)

hear and voice
at Sinai
Deut. 4:12, 30, 33,
36; 5:20, 21, 22, 23,
25, 25

53 That God reveals Himself through the aspect of *voice* is self-evident in the account of the revelation at Sinai: "a *voice* of words did you hear, but a form you did not see, only a *voice*" (Deut. 4:12). "Behold ... we have heard His *voice* out of the midst of the fire" (5:21).

54 These mark the *first* and *seventh* times, respectively, that the expression "send/sent forth his hand (שלח ידו)" appears in the Torah, and the *seventh* reflects the *first*. At Sinai, they partook of the Tree of Life, the Torah, and God did not "send forth his hand." (Excluded in this count is "send forth *your/their/my hand*" [Gen. 19:10; 22:12; Ex. 3:20; 4:4; 9:15].)

sent שלח ידו
forth his hand
Gen. 3:22; 8:9;
22:10; Ex. 4:4;
22:7, 10; 24:11

55 See U. Cassuto to Ex. 24:5–11, *A Commentary on the Book of Exodus* (Jerusalem: Magnes Press, 1951 [first English edition, 1967]), 311–315.

56 *The Zohar*, translated by Harry Sperling and Maurice Simon, (London: Soncino Press, 1934), 165.

57 What right have we to associate Rebekah's *voice* with the *Voice* of God? Could Rebekah's *voice* be connected more to the *voice* of Eve than to the *Voice* of God? Let us compare texts:

And to Adam He said: "Because you *have hearkened to the voice* of your wife, *and have eaten* from the tree *of which I commanded you,* saying, 'You shall *not eat* of it,' *cursed* is the ground for your sake; in toil shall you eat of it." (Gen. 3:17)

And Rebekah spoke to Jacob her son, saying, "And now, my son, *hearken to my voice to that which I command you.* Go now to the flock, and fetch me two good kids of the goats; and I will make of them savory food for your father, such as he loves. *And he will eat,* so that he may *bless* you before his death." (27:6–10)

The two texts have many contrasting parallels. Eve's beckoning led to a *curse*, but Rebekah's counsel led to a *blessing*. Adam heeded Eve's call to disobey a *command*, while Rebekah urged Jacob to obey a *command*. Adam and Eve "hid from the presence of the LORD" (Gen. 3:8). In contrast, Isaac's soul became attached to the Source of blessing (see Malbim to 27:10 and 27:21). Adam and Eve ate fruit from the Tree of the Knowledge of *Good* and *Evil*, but Isaac ate savory food made from "*two good* kids of the goats" (27:9), from the *good within the good*. This was no ordinary food that Isaac ate, but *tasty food* (מַטְעַמִּים) like the manna from heaven whose "*taste* (טעמו) was as the *taste* (כטעם) of fresh oil" (Num. 11:8). (The root טעם appears only in Num. 11:8, in Ex. 16:31 in relation to the manna, and in Gen. 27:4, 7, 9, 14, 17, 31). The *voice* of Eve had led man out of the Garden, but the inner *voice* of Rebekah would return man onto the path that leads to the Tree of Life.

58 Esau, too, "did eat (ויאכל), and did *drink* (וישת)," but "he rose up and went his way, and so Esau despised his birthright" (Gen. 25:34). Unlike the descendants of Jacob who *ate* and *drank* while accepting the Torah (Ex. 24:11), Esau ate and *drank* while shunning this spiritual heritage of Abraham.

59 Rabbi Menachem Schneerson notes: ". . . Jacob is compared to Adam [*Bava Batra* 58a], and he corrected the latter's sin, as explained in the works of the Kabbalah [see *Iggeret Hakodesh,* section VII, and nn. 22–23 in the English translation]. Adam had been misled by the *mirma* (cunning) of the serpent. Hence, in order to correct this, and to prevent the blessing from being passed to Esau, Jacob had to procure them by means of *mirma*: 'Your brother came with *mirma,* and he has taken your blessing' [Gen. 27:35]," M. Schneerson, *op. cit.,* 105–105.

60 See Malbim to Gen. 27:1 and 27:4, where he notes that Rebekah "was fully aware of how Yizhaq wanted to create a bond between Esav and Ya'aqov . . . Ya'aqov would pursue Torah, while Esav would provide him with sustenance. However, Rivqa knew all too well Esav's wickedness. . . . Not only would he not protect him, as the shell protects the moth but, like decay, he would cause everything to perish. The wealth that his father would bestow upon him through his blessing he would keep to himself, and use it to harm Ya'aqov." Translation from Zvi Faier, *Malbim, Commentary on the Torah, Book Two: The Patriarchs* (Jerusalem: Hillel Press, 1979), 363.

61 Jacob feared that he might have sinned, thereby forfeiting God's protection. Similarly, God's promise of uplift to Cain depended on Cain doing good and keeping away from sin.

Eber עבר
10:21, 24, 25; 11:14, 15, 16, 17

62 These letters also spell the name of Shem's son, *Eber* (עבר), which appears *seven* times prior to Gen. 32:22. The conjunction בַּעֲבוּר or בְּעֶבֶר, rendered *for the sake of, on account of, in order that,* occurs *fourteen* times from the beginning of the Torah

to our verse. The *Hebrew* (הָעִבְרִי), having an extra letter *yud* at the end, occurs one time (14:13).

There is another interesting word count link to our verse:

Hashem *passed over before his face* (וַיַּעֲבֹר יְהוָה עַל־פָּנָיו) and proclaimed: "Hashem! Hashem! God compassionate and gracious, slow to anger, abounding in kindness and faithfulness. (Ex. 34:6)

In both Gen. 32:22 and Ex. 34:6, we find the expression, *passed over . . . before his face*. In the literary section defined by these verses (Gen. 32:22–Ex. 34:6), *his face* (פניו) occurs exactly *seven* times. The expression *before his face* (עַל־פָּנָיו) occurs at both the beginning and the end of this textual unit. As brother shares blessing with brother, Divine blessing flows down upon man.

63 Does not include prefixes added to פניו, such as לפניו or מפניו.

64 The next time עַל־פָּנָיו appears in the Torah is in Ex. 34:6: "Hashem passed before him and proclaimed: Hashem! Hashem! A God compassionate and gracious, slow to anger, abounding in kindness and faithfulness." Exodus 34:6 marks the *seventh* time in the Torah for various expressions of *on his/my/your face*.

65 In the remainder of the section, if we exclude the name *Peniel* (פנואל), we find the root of the word *face* (פנה) an additional *seven* times. However, if we include the name *Peniel* (lit. *face of God*, פניאל), then we have another interesting unit of seven, wherein the *seventh* reflects the *first*. This unit begins with:

And Jacob called the name of the place *Peniel* (*face of God*); for I have seen God *face* to *face*, and my life is preserved. (32:31)

The unit ends with:

for as much as I have seen your *face*, as one sees the *face of God*, and you have been gracious to me. (33:10)

Both the *first* and the *seventh* of this unit contain a reference to *face of God*. This symmetry forms a nexus between the *face* of the angel, with whom Jacob wrestled, and the face of his brother, lending force to Rashi, who says Jacob had encountered Esau's guardian angel (Rashi to 33:10). Alternatively, Jacob had reached the level where he could see the image of God in the face of his brother.

66 This is an oversimplification, since some words are more likely to appear than others.

67 For a discussion of entropy and Torah, see Z. Faier's notes to his English translation of *Malbim, Commentary on the Torah, Book One, Beginning and Upheaval* (Jerusalem: Hillel Press, 1978), 125–138.

68 This verse (Gen. 4:3), which contains the first occurrence of *offering* in the Torah, has *thirty-six* letters, that is, *six* times *six*, a perfect sexagesimal number. The verse containing the *seventh* appearance of *offering* (32:22) has *thirty-six* letters, too. This numerical symmetry adds additional strength to the bond between these two verses.

69 This opening verse of the Cain and Abel narrative (Gen. 4:1) has exactly *fourteen* words and *forty-nine* letters (*seven* times *seven*).

70 Both of these verses (Gen. 4:2 and 25:27) have *fourteen* words.

בעבור
for the sake of
3:17; 8:21; 12:13,
16; 18:26, 29, 31,
32; 21:30; 26:24;
27:4, 10, 19, 31

his face פניו
Gen. 32:22; 43:31,
34; Ex. 3:6; 28:25,
27; 34:6

on his/my/ your face
Gen. 17:3, 17;
32:22; Ex. 20:3,
20; 33:19; 34:6

face פנה
Gen. 32:31; 31;
33:3, 10, 10, 14, 14

Peniel פניאל
32:31, 31, 31, 32;
33:3, 10, 10

71 Rashi's comment to Gen. 32:11: "*I am unworthy of all the kindness:* My merits are diminished in consequence of all the kindness and truth which You have already shown me; For this reason I am afraid; perhaps, since You made these promises to me, I have become corrupted by sin, and this may cause me to be delivered unto Esau."

72 *Desire* (שׁוק) appears only twice in the Torah (Gen. 3:16 and 4:7).

73 The Malbim notes that the act of *kissing* joins spirit to spirit so that the uppermost blessing can flow down. In spite of the deception, the *kiss* was efficacious. After the *kiss*, Isaac's blessing follows immediately, as the *kiss* joins the spirit of Jacob to the spirit of Isaac.

74 Corresponding to, "And the first one came out red (אדמוני)" (Gen. 25:25). Rashi comments, "This is a sign he will shed blood."

75 See Rashi to Gen. 32:11.

76 Malbim, Faier, *op. cit.*, 301–302.

77 In his classic work, *Duties of the Heart*, R. Bachya ibn Paquda writes: "None of the created things can benefit or hurt either itself or any other creature, save with the blessed Creator's permission." In addition, "God's control is complete in all these things. In none can any human being plan aught or exercise any control, save with the Almighty's permission, decree and ordinance. . . . A human being's end and length of his days on earth are determined by the blessed Creator's decree." R. Bachya ben Joseph ibn Paquda, *Duties of the Heart, Vol. I*, with English translation by Moses Hyamson, (Jerusalem/New York: Feldheim Publishers, 1970 [paperback edition 1978]), 305, 325.

78 As we noted in the first chapter, *six* represents the physical world, as in the *six* days of Creation. *Seven* symbolizes the spiritual aspect of Creation, as well as completion and perfection, as in the Sabbath Day. *Eight* is one level above seven, that which is beyond time and space.

79 When the dawn rises, Esau has already received Jacob's offering. It is written: "And the sun rose upon him as he passed over Penuel . . . And Jacob lifted his eyes, and, behold, Esau was coming" (Gen. 32:32–33:1). Also, "What do you mean by all this company which I have met?" (33:8). Esau received Jacob's offering during the night.

80 As pointed out to me by Rabbi Murray Schaum, *and he restrained himself* (ויתאפק) is linguistically similar to *and he wrestled* (ויאבק) (Gen. 32:25). The letter *bet* (ב) and the *pay* (פ) have the same sound, except that one is vocalized with the voice box, and the other is not. Perhaps, Joseph's inner struggle, as he tries to hold back his tears in the presence of his brothers, is connected to Jacob's inner struggle, as he wrestles with the angel. Joseph needs to seek reconciliation, instead of vengeance.

81 Gen. 1:2, 2, 20, 29; 2:6; 3:8; 4:5 (the seventh: "And Cain was very angry, and his *face* fell"), 6, 14, 14, 16; 6:1, 7, 11, 13, 13; 7:1, 3, 4, 7, 18 (the twenty-first: "and the ark went upon the *face* of the waters"), 23; 8:8, 9, 13; 9:23; 10:9, 9; 11:4, 8, 9, 28; 13:9, 10; 16:6, 8, 12; 17:1, 3, 17, 18; 18:8, 16, 22, 22; 19:13, 21, 27, 28, 28; 20:15; 23:3, 4, 8, 12, 17, 19; 24:7, 12, 31, 33, 40, 49, 51, 63; 25: 9, 18, 18; 27:7, 7, 10, 20, 30, 46; 29:26; 30:30, 33, 40; 31:2, 5, 21, 35; 32:4, 17, 18, 21, 21, 21, 21, 22 (the ninetieth) [90 = 60 + 60/2, a

sexigesimal number].

82 *Thirteen* – the numerical equivalent of the word *one* (אחד) – is a combination of six and seven, the unity of the physical world and the spiritual. As such, *thirteen times seven* (91) is a number of great spiritual elevation.

83 This verse (Gen. 1:2) has 52 (4 × 13, or 2 × 26) letters. The verse containing the 13 × 7th *face*, "And Jacob called the name of the place Peniel, for I have seen God *face to face*, and my life is preserved" (Gen. 32:31) has 52 letters, also.

84 These three verses have 15 words (3 + 5 + 7) and 60 letters (15 + 20 + 25), displaying a numerical progression for words and letters.

85 This is the *seventh* of the *seven* appearances of שם (*there/name*) in the chapter.

86 This marks the *eighth* of the *eight* appearances in the chapter of the root of *pass over* (עבר).

87 The word *night* appears in the Sodom and Gomorra story four times (Gen. 19:5, 33, 34, 35), including two as *that night* (בלילה הוא). Also, we find the first two occurrences of *lodge* (לין) in this same chapter (19:2, 2), another key word from Gen. 32:22.

88 This marks the *eighth* time the root of the word *whole/peace* (שלם) appears in the Torah. The end of the verse, ". . . and he encamped *in the face of* (את־פני) the city," marks the 100th appearance of the root of the word *face* in the Torah.

89 We find the word *pass over* (עבר) used to describe Abraham's arrival in the land of Canaan at the city of Shechem (Gen. 12:6). Compare the use of the words *took*, *wife*, came, *land of Canaan*, *pass over*, and *Shechem* with Abraham (12:1–6) and with Jacob (32:23–25; 33:18). For Abraham, the verb *pass over* (עבר) is used to indicate a transformation from the idolatry of his father to the belief in one God. See, also, the book of Joshua, wherein the Children of Israel *pass over* the Jordan River into the Promised Land (Josh. 1:2; 3:17). It is interesting that many of the words in our verse (Gen. 32:22) are found in the first few chapters of Joshua: *night* (1:8; 2:2; 4:3), *camp* (1:11; 3:2, 5:8), *lodge* (3:1, 4:3, 3, 8), and numerous uses of the word *face* and *pass over*.

90 *ArtScroll Tenach Series/Bereishis, Vol. 4* (Brooklyn: Mesorah Publications, 1979), 1384.

91 Also, ". . . the signs and wonders that the Lord sent him *to make* (לַעֲשׂוֹת) in the land of Egypt" (Deut. 34:11), which include the ten plagues, struck at the ten sayings of Creation, "which God created to make (לַעֲשׂוֹת)" (Gen. 2:2), demonstrating God's mastery over all aspects of the natural world.

92 The sevenfold symmetry of God (אלקים) comes on Day Seven, where that Name is enscribed for the 35th time.

93 As noted earlier, יצחק recurs 100 times, twice as the meaning of his name, *he will laugh*, and 98 times (2 × 7²) referring to his actual name, *Isaac*. Our counting deals with the exact word, יצחק, regardless of the meaning in the context. The letters that form the name of the Patriarch total 100 in the Torah.

94 Particles can be produced that are entangled, with each having the opposite state of the other, such as an up or down spin. It is indeterminable which of these entangled pairs has an up spin and which has a down spin. Their mutual states are

there/name שם
Gen. 32:3, 28, 29, 30, 30, 30, 31

pass over עבר
Gen. 32:11, 17, 22, 23, 23, 24, 24, 32

שלם
whole/peace
Gen. 15:15, 16; 26:29, 31; 28:21; 29:6, 6; 33:18

uncertain, except for the fact that they are opposite to each other. Before they are measured, each particle exists having both up and down spins at the same time – a superposition (a mixing of possible states). This has been proven experimentally. Once the state of one of the particles is measured – up or down spin – the superposition collapses and the entangled partner assumes the opposite state, even when great distances separate the particles (Kenneth W. Ford, *The Quantum World: Quantum Physics for Everyone*, [Harvard University Press, 2004], 231).

95 Benjamin Schumacher, *Quantum Mechanics: The Physics of the Microscopic World*, (The Teaching Company, 2009), 55. See also Ford, *op. cit.*, 227–240; and Fred Alan Brown, *Taking the Quantum Leap*, (Harper & Row, 1981), 168–189.

96 Intertextual entanglement is not limited to numerical symmetries based upon the number seven.

97 From Walt Whitman's *Song of Myself*, found in *Leaves of Grass*. ("Owners" and "Whose" were changed to uppercase by the author.)